CHAK

NAOMI OZANIEC ... field of spirituality for almost 25 years following a power... ...ce in 1975. Since then she has been involved in a num... ...groups. In the late 70s she ran groups under the aegis of the Green Circle. During the 80s she worked with Dolores Ashcroft-Nowicki and Gareth Knight, learning the potence of applied sacred psychology. In 1990 she was invited to take ordination with Olivia Durdin-Robertson of the fellowship of Isis. In 1993 Naomi was a delegate for the Fellowship at the World Parliament of Religions. She is currently working in partnership with the artist Stuart Littlejohn to restore the spirit of the House of Life as a vehicle for the sacred as both art and word.

New Perspectives

THE SERIES

New Perspectives provide attractive and accessible introductions to a comprehensive range of mind, body and spirit topics. Beautifully designed and illustrated, these practical books are written by experts in each subject.

Titles in the series include:

ASTROLOGY
by Janis Huntley

BUDDHISM
by John Snelling

CHAKRAS
by Naomi Ozaniec

COLOUR THERAPY
by Pauline Wills

CRYSTAL THERAPY
by Stephanie Harrison & Tim Harrison

HERBAL REMEDIES
by Vicki Pitman

I CHING
by Stephen Karcher

NUTRITIONAL THERAPY
by Jeannette Ewin

RUNES
by Bernard King

SHAMANISM
by Nevill Drury

TAI CHI
by Paul Crompton

YOGA
by Howard Kent

New Perspectives

CHAKRAS

An Introductory Guide to Your Energy Centres for Total Health

NAOMI OZANIEC

ELEMENT

Shaftesbury, Dorset • Boston, Massachusetts
Melbourne, Victoria

First published as The Elements of Chakras in 1996 by
Element Books Limited
This revised edition first published in Great Britain in 2000 by
Element Books Limited, Shaftesbury, Dorset SP7 8BP

Published in the USA in 2000 by
Element Books, Inc.
160 North Washington Street,
Boston, MA 02114

Published in Australia in 2000 by
Element Books and distributed by
Penguin Australia Limited,
487 Maroondah Highway, Ringwood,
Victoria 3134

Designed for Element Books Limited by
Design Revolution, Queens Park Villa,
30 West Drive, Brighton, East Sussex BN2 2GE

ELEMENT BOOKS LIMITED
Editorial Director: Sarah Sutton
Project Editor: Kelly Wakely
Commissioning Editor: Grace Cheetham
Production Director: Roger Lane

DESIGN REVOLUTION
Editorial Director: Ian Whitelaw
Art Director: Lindsey Johns
Project Editor: Nicola Hodgson
Editor: Susie Behar
Designer: Vanessa Good

Printed and bound in Great Britain by
Bemrose Security Printing, Derby

British Library Cataloguing in Publication
Data available

Library of Congress Cataloging in Publication
Data available

ISBN 1-86204-765-0

CONTENTS

ACKNOWLEDGEMENTS

The publishers wish to thank AKG London Picture Library for the use of pictures on pages 8 and 109.

INTRODUCTION

This book is no more than an introduction to a vast area of knowledge that is available on the centres of energy in the body, known as chakras. It provides an intellectual framework and some practical guidelines for working with the energy of the chakras in your own life. If you decide to implement the exercises indicated, it is absolutely vital that you do not rush through them. Do not anticipate spectacular results. The changes should be gently transformative. You should become more aware of how you draw upon the chakra energies in your life, which ones you spontaneously relate to and which ones seem more distant. Your practice will need to be regular; meditation, pranayama and physical work should be incorporated into your everyday life. This requires a high level of commitment. What you get from your work will be directly proportional to what you put in.

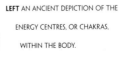

LEFT AN ANCIENT DEPICTION OF THE ENERGY CENTRES, OR CHAKRAS, WITHIN THE BODY.

The book contains sufficient suggestions for you to devise your own programme of work for each of the chakras. You can quite safely combine the affirmations, Bach flower remedies, suitable music and the preliminary exercises. Doing this will orient your mind towards the appropriate chakra. The more advanced techniques of asanas and pranayama are without doubt more demanding. If you feel that these techniques are beyond your capacity or requirement. Follow your instincts and wait until you are ready to take on these disciplines.

Ultimate success will depend upon you. The spirit in which you approach this work is critical. Idle curiosity, or pure academic interest will yield only a poor harvest. From the outset you need a deep commitment and the ability to persevere. Certain people find conscious awakening only too easy; others find it slow, laborious and fraught. Karmic factors are possibly the most significant in determining both our capacity and strength of determination. In the absence of a teacher who might be able to detect the karmic factors involved, strength of feeling is a good rough guide of spiritual aspiration. If you have the motivation and willingness to undertake a course of spiritual study and application, you will reap your own reward.

Anyone involved in their own spiritual awakening through yoga, psychic development or

LEFT TO AWAKEN THE CHAKRAS, A PERSON NEEDS TO DEVELOP SPIRITUAL AWARENESS THROUGH PRACTICES SUCH AS YOGA AND MEDITATION.

metaphysical training of any kind is already working with the chakras. Anyone working as a medium, a psychic, a healer, or spiritual practitioner of whatever persuasion is also working with these living energies. Knowledge in this instance can be helpful and indeed absolutely necessary at times. There seems to be a general lack of understanding about the chakras even in Western esoteric circles. I have often encountered the attitude that chakras are 'Eastern things', as if Westerners did not have chakras. Everyone has chakras.

The undeniable spiritual impetus within the West is giving rise to a new eclectic and dynamic tradition. This new tradition draws from many sources and incorporates spiritual, psychological and therapeutic aspects. It is keenly focused on the problems of the real world and has a deep commitment to rediscovering spiritual realities. Knowledge of the chakras will surely be safe in these hands; I hope this proves to be so.

THE LANDSCAPE OF SUBTLE ENERGIES

'Chakra' is a Sanskrit word meaning wheel. A wheel spins on its own axis; it can turn slowly or rapidly. Like the coloured disks that children spin on a length of thread, a chakra spins in relation to the degree of energy in the system. The wheel itself is a powerful symbol representing the many cyclic patterns of life. It is rather curious to find that this ancient and foreign term is now fully integrated into New Age vocabulary. As so often is the case these days, what appears to be 'New Age', is in reality, extremely 'Old Age'. The chakras evolve naturally over a long period of time as part of the development of the whole person. Some spiritual systems seek to educate the whole being, knowing that the chakras will change accordingly. It is also possible to quicken the pace of opening and to accelerate this evolutionary process. Other spiritual systems seek to awaken the chakras, knowing that this will accordingly affect the whole being.

LEFT A CHAKRA CAN BE THOUGHT OF AS A WHEEL OR CIRCLE OF ENERGY THAT SPINS WITHIN THE BODY.

THE LOTUS FLOWER

Chakras are also known as lotuses or padmas. This beautiful symbol tells us a great deal about the nature of the chakra as a living force. The lotus, which is not unlike a water lily, blooms upon the water but its roots are deeply buried in the mud far below the surface. It has come to represent the human condition. It is rooted in the mud and darkness of the depths but ultimately it flowers under the light of the sun. Just like a lotus, the chakra can be closed, in bud, opening, active or dormant.

LEFT THE LOTUS FLOWER, WHICH GROWS IN ASIA. IS OFTEN USED TO REPRESENT CHAKRAS.

11

Where are the chakras? They are to be found within each of us. Just as everyone has a physical body, so, too does everyone also have a subtle body. The chakras serve as a bridging mechanism between physical matter and subtle matter.

We find information about the chakras most notably in Hindu canonical literature in the Upanishads. The Hindu tradition is a rich source of information and inspiration. It furnishes us with descriptions, representations and practical techniques for chakra work. The spiritual initiates of this tradition worked extensively with these energies and left a rich heritage of paintings, symbolic images, cosmograms, meditations and texts.

RIGHT THE HINDU GOD PARVATI. INFORMATION ABOUT CHAKRAS CAN BE FOUND IN ANCIENT HINDU LITERATURE.

We find teachings concerning the chakras in many other major spiritual traditions. Within Tibetan Buddhism, knowledge of the chakras is thoroughly integrated into practice. The centres are called channel wheels. They are used extensively in certain significant visualizations by the practitioner. Taoist yoga is a complex discipline based upon the control and circulation of vital energies. The Western alchemical tradition had a deep understanding of the chakras. Metals and planets were assigned to the chakras in an elaborate system of correspondences that formed the basis of the alchemists' approach to the quest for spiritual transformation. With the decline of the alchemical arts, codified knowledge about the chakras faded in the West.

THE CHAKRAS AND SUBTLE ANATOMY

12

The chakras themselves are part of a greater network of subtle energies. We cannot isolate them without violating holistic principles. Our physical make-up is well researched and documented through the many body-based sciences. Our subtle make-up can only be explored through quite different means: involvement rather than clinical detachment, and a holistic frame of reference. However, the physical and the non-physical aspects of being are two aspects of the same whole; they cannot really be separated. We cannot study subtle anatomy without seeing its relationship to physical anatomy. Equally, physical anatomy without knowledge of subtle anatomy is incomplete.

The idea that living cells, whether in human, animal or vegetable form, radiate an invisible presence has been an enduring concept. The development of Kirlian photography has now revealed the reality of life energy for the first time. It is possible to see energy flows and emanations from quite simple life forms captured in beautiful photographic form. This technique has revealed the reality of non-physical energies quite clearly. If we are now able to catch a glimpse of the emanations from simple cell structures such as plants and even vegetables, we can only wonder what intricate energy patterns conscious and complicated human beings might radiate.

Simple aggregations of living tissue generate a luminescence. It is therefore likely that more specialized groups of cells arranged into physical organs will give rise to more organized energy patterns. Stop for a moment and list the body's major systems. Your list will probably include cognition, respiration, circulation, digestion, reproduction and excretion. Their equivalents are the six chakras of awakening. The brain, not surprisingly, has an additional centre giving a total of seven major chakras. These are located over the top of the head, over the brow at the centre of the forehead, at the throat, at the heart, at the solar plexus, at the sexual centre and at the base of the body (*see* p.14).

THE CHAKRAS AND THE PHYSICAL BODY

Each chakra corresponds to certain physical systems and the related organs. The base chakra relates to the large intestine and the rectum. It also shares some responsibility for the functions of the kidneys, which rid the body of waste matter. The sacral chakra relates to the reproductive system, ovaries and testes, the bladder and the kidneys. The solar plexus chakra relates to the liver, gall bladder, stomach, spleen and small intestine. The heart chakra relates to the heart and the arms. The throat chakra relates to the lungs and throat. The brow chakra relates to the brain. The crown chakra is not limited to one part of the body, but relates to the whole being.

There is a direct relationship between the condition of the chakra and the corresponding physical organs. A chakra can be over-vitalized, under-vitalized or in a state of balance. It can be open or blocked. Dysfunction, for example, of the reproductive system will usually manifest with obvious physical symptoms such as disrupted

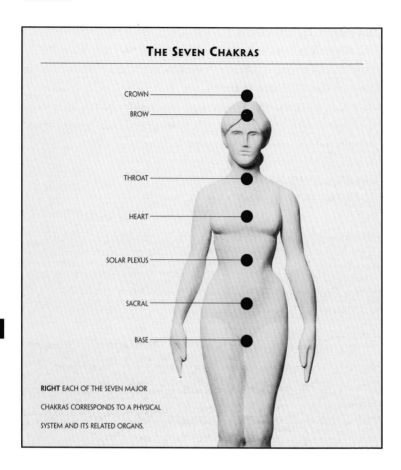

THE SEVEN CHAKRAS

CROWN

BROW

THROAT

HEART

SOLAR PLEXUS

SACRAL

BASE

RIGHT EACH OF THE SEVEN MAJOR
CHAKRAS CORRESPONDS TO A PHYSICAL
SYSTEM AND ITS RELATED ORGANS.

14

menstruation. The physical symptoms will be mirrored by dysfunction within the related energy network and the chakra itself. Creating change to restore the related energy system to a state of balance will create change at the physical level.

CHAKRAS AND THE GLANDS

The chakras function as transmuters of energy from one level to another, distributing pranic energy to the physical body. This is done in part through the glands which regulate different systems within the body. Traditionally each of the chakras is also related to a major gland.

The base chakra is related to the adrenals; the sacral chakra is related to the ovaries in women and the testes in men; the solar plexus chakra is related to the pancreas; the heart chakra is related to the thymus; the throat chakra is related to the thyroid and parathryroid glands; the brow chakra is most often assigned to the pituitary gland, sometimes to the pineal; and the crown chakra is most often assigned to the pineal gland, sometimes to the pituitary gland.

MAINTAINING HEALTH

The endocrine glands play a vital role in the everyday health and well-being of the body. The hormones released directly into the bloodstream by the glands govern all aspects of growth, development and daily physical activity.

Dysfunction by any of the endocrine glands will have serious physical consequences. Physical malfunction is itself the result of a breakdown that becomes lodged within the energy network of nadis (the channels that conduct pranic energy) and chakras.

The number of chakras sometimes varies from one tradition to another. This is not a cause for disagreement but rather a question of accounting. There are two subsidiary centres allied to the heart and

15

THE CHAKRAS AND THE PHYSICAL BODY

CHAKRA	LOCATION	GLAND
Muladhara	Coccygeal Plexus	Adrenals
Svadisthana	Sacral Plexus	Testes/Ovaries
Manipura	Solar Plexus	Pancreas
Anahata	Cardiac Plexus	Thymus
Vishuddha	Cervical Plexus	Thyroid/Parathyroid
Ajna	Cavernous Plexus	Pituitary
Sahasrara	Meridian Plexus	Pineal

THE CHAKRAS AND THE ENDOCRINE SYSTEM

CHAKRA 7 – PINEAL GLAND

CHAKRA 6 – PITUITARY GLAND

CHAKRA 5 – THYROID GLAND
AND PARATHYROID

CHAKRA 4 – THYMUS GLAND

CHAKRA 1 – ADRENAL
GLANDS

CHAKRA 3 – PANCREAS

ACUPUNCTURE POINTS

CHAKRA 2 – OVARIES

ABOVE THE ENDOCRINE
SYSTEM IS VERY IMPORTANT
IN MAINTAINING THE
BODY'S HEALTH. EACH
GLAND IN THE SYSTEM IS
RELATED TO A CHAKRA.

throat chakras. Some authorities do not include the centre at the top of the head as a chakra, treating it instead as a unique centre of consciousness. The number of chakras given can therefore vary from six up to nine. The number most often given is seven: the six chakras of awakening and the crown chakra at the top of the head.

THE SUSHUMNA, IDA AND PINGALA MERIDIANS

Just as the physical body is far more than just a collection of organs, the subtle vehicle is far more than a collection of chakras. The physical organs are connected as part of a greater whole, and the chakras are also connected as part of a greater whole. The body has other vital systems without which it could not function: it has a complicated network of nerves, centralized in the spinal column, highly developed senses and a vitally important system of hormone regulators. The subtle vehicle also has other vital systems: there is a network of interconnecting energy channels called meridians or nadis (the word 'nad' means to flow). There are a number of major channels also called meridians and a vast number of increasingly finer minor ones.

THE SUSHUMNA

Within the physical body the spine is of great importance and the spine also has a vital part to play in the circulation of subtle energies. The sushumna, which is the most important of the nadis, rises within the base chakra following the spine. It terminates at the crown chakra, the Gate of Brahman. The sushumna nadi is also known as the channel of fire or Sarasvati, one of India's sacred rivers. Sushumna itself is three-fold in nature, containing finer forces arranged one within the other. The innermost of these is citrini, 'The Heavenly Way, this is the giver of the joy of immortality'. This current is equilibrating by nature.

THE SUSHUMNA/GOVERNING VESSEL MERIDIAN

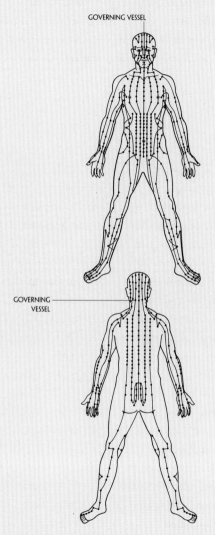

GOVERNING VESSEL

GOVERNING VESSEL

ABOVE THE SUSHUMNA MERIDIAN IS VERY SIMILAR TO THE GOVERNING VESSEL MERIDIAN, ONE OF 14 MAIN MERIDIANS IN THE SYSTEM OF ACUPUNCTURE.

Next comes vajra; its nature is active and forceful. The outer channel is sushumna; its natural tendency is towards inertia and inactivity. The chakras are rooted upon citrini but open upon the surface of the appropriate energy field. Alice Bailey describes the sushumna as being composed of the forces of life, consciousness and creativity. It bears a remarkable resemblance to the governor vessel meridian, which rises at the tip of the coccyx, travels up the centre of the back and passes over the back of the head to finish at the upper lip. This is a major meridian in acupuncture.

IDA AND PINGALA

In addition to the sushumna there are two other important channels; ida and pingala. Ida is also called chandra, the moon or the Ganges River, while pingala is also known as surya, the sun or the Yamuna River. The pingala nadi emerges from the right side of the base chakra and travels up the body in a series of curves crossing back and forth over the sushumna. The ida nadi emerges from the left side of the base chakra and travels up the body, creating the other half of a symmetrical pattern. Ida, pingala and sushumna meet at the brow centre between the eyebrows and form a plaited knot of energies. From here the three rivers Ganges, Yamuna and Sarasvati flow as a single current. The pattern they make has been likened to a pair of intertwined serpents. Some authorities indicate that ida and pingala form a pattern that passes around the chakras. Other authorities, including Swami Saytananda, indicate that the chakras emerge at the junctions where ida and pingala cross sushumna.

In my dowsing work I have noted that the left and the right side of a healthy body produce clockwise and counter-clockwise flows of energy. This effect seems to be connected to the polarity of the body, which is primarily established through the two hemispheres of the brain. The chakras fall upon the central line of the body and rotate in various clockwise and counter-clockwise combinations. Moving slightly left of centre (ida) we encounter a swirl moving in a

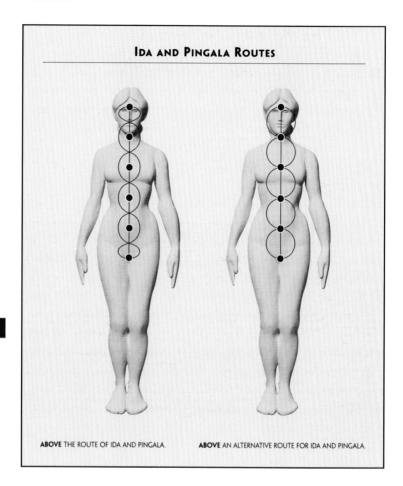

IDA AND PINGALA ROUTES

ABOVE THE ROUTE OF IDA AND PINGALA.   **ABOVE** AN ALTERNATIVE ROUTE FOR IDA AND PINGALA.

20

clockwise direction. Moving slightly right of centre we encounter a swirl moving in a counter-clockwise direction. When we combine these two patterns the spiral image naturally emerges as we pass up the body. This same pattern appears as we travel up the back. Any disturbance of this spiral pattern is indicative of the symptoms of localized illness.

Ida and pingala are the polar forces that are generated by the two hemispheres of the brain. This network is anchored at either end of the circuit at the base and brow centres.

THE KUNDALINI EXPERIENCE

The spinal network of energies is a vital part of the subtle anatomy of the human individual. The chakras are strung upon the inner column of sushumna like jewels on a necklace. It is this central column which unifies the separated chakras into a whole. It is possible for high levels of energy to rise up from the base chakra through the spinal nadi and dramatically affect all the chakras simultaneously. This force is latent but can be stimulated by work that awakens the chakras individually. The Kundalini force is like a coiled spring. In fact Kundalini is most often depicted in a coiled form as a sleeping serpent. Kundalini shakti can rise and retreat again many times before completing the journey to the top chakra. We cannot understand the chakras individually without considering them as a unified whole, as aspects of a single power.

When the latent power awakens, the ensuing experience can take many forms dependent upon the consciousness of the practitioner. It can be frightening, bewildering, dramatic and disturbing, hardly ever gentle. The full Kundalini experience brings reconstruction of total being. It can be likened to a living second birth with all the accompanying birth trauma. I like to think of it as a quantum leap.

THE AURA

The five senses serve the physical self sufficiently well. Yet esoteric traditions have long taught that both the five senses and the physical form are limited and incomplete expressions of total reality. The physical body is surrounded by an ovoid emanation. It is made up of different bands of energy which each reflect an aspect of being. The innermost band follows the outline of the body. This is the etheric body. Beyond this is a band of finer substance which reflects the emotional nature. It is usually called the astral body or sometimes the

desire body. Beyond this still lies the mental body, a level of emanation which reflects the mental nature. Together these bands of energy form the aura, the mirror of being. The aura can be seen through clairvoyant vision in terms of colour, brightness, clarity and definition.

THE ETHERIC FIELD

The belief that we are not purely physical beings is universally held within living spiritual traditions. Such a belief is intimately connected to a wider view of reality. Accordingly the physical form is viewed as one manifestation of total being. It is regarded as the most dense vehicle of consciousness, composed of matter vibrating within certain frequencies. As Kirlian photography has shown us, living cells generate a non-physical luminescence or emanation which interpenetrates and surrounds the organic whole, whether it is vegetable, plant, animal or human. This is the etheric vehicle, sheath, body or field, depending on terminology. It is very easy to feel this energy field through quite basic exercise. This level of vibration is sometimes referred to as the health aura or vital body, as patterns of disease appear first within the etheric form. The physical and etheric levels serve as a unified whole.

The physical sheath is called annamaya kosha in the Upanishads. The etheric vehicle is called pranamaya kosha. Together these two levels are called the atma puri, the city of the soul. Both the physical and the etheric vehicles need prana for the maintenance of health and vitality. The physical body draws mainly upon gross prana provided by food and the air. It also draws upon some degree of subtle prana. The etheric form transmutes subtle prana from more refined levels and transmutes it via the chakras. The etheric level, in contrast to the physical, is highly sensitive to thought patterns, and so the surrounding etheric double can be expanded through visualization and directed breathing.

THE ASTRAL FIELD

Next we encounter what is commonly called the astral or emotional body. This is also called the desire body as this level reflects our true desires. This band of emanation extends some distance beyond the body in all directions. We might also like to think of it as a system of personal antennae. When we meet someone for the first time or find ourselves in a strange place, the astral field picks up and transmits sensations to us. We can feel uncomfortable or ill at ease in what appears to be a perfectly acceptable situation. We can sense something about another person long before we are able to confirm this. When two people are attracted, the two energy fields blend or merge by extending towards each other. Conversely, anger and strong feelings of dislike create barriers between the fields: there is no merging or interaction; the two energy fields remain closed.

There is a constant play of energies as the astral field mirrors all changes of mood and responds to the moods and vibrations of others. Human emotions generate specific patterns of energy: hatred, lust, greed, desire, anger, love, devotion – each possesses different vibrations. The astral form reflects the interplay of emotions like a mirror. Its clarity and quality directly reflect the emotional responses. Those with clairvoyant vision indicate that brightness and light accompany the selfless range of emotions such as compassion and altruistic love. The astral sheath can be dark, leaden and even distorted, mirroring persistent ugly emotional states.

THE MAGIC MIRROR

The magic mirror is a favourite image in fairy-tales. It symbolizes the living astral mirror which truthfully reveals desires. The astral field mirrors without discrimination. In children, because the mental field is undeveloped, the astral field opens directly onto the outside world. Adults who have not brought the emotions under mental control remain polarised at this level. If the emotional field is to be aligned to spiritual purpose, a quiet mind, self-awareness and spiritual aspiration need to be nurtured to counter the bias of subjective feeling and the reactive response. Buddhism lays great stress on the development of equanimity as a means of countering the extreme and unbalanced feelings produced by the unrestrained play of the emotions. Personal desires and motives are brought into consciousness and raised to their highest expression through all-embracing compassion.

24 THE MENTAL FIELD

The mental sheath constitutes the outer and least dense aspect of the aura. It appears to begin at the edge of the astral field, although in fact it interpenetrates all astral, etheric and physical substance. This band of energy reflects the mental nature and develops with the ability to use the mind in certain ways. The range of mental activities which our society requires through education and work rarely stimulates development at this level. Alice Bailey outlines the types of activity that sharpen the mental aura. She claims that the individual needs to develop the ability to think clearly on 'all matters affecting the race'. This seems a tall order, but it raises all the fundamental questions that most people seek to avoid, and sets the level for abstract thought. The mind has to be focused through the practice of concentration, comprehended through the practice of meditation and raised to its highest through contemplation. With the development of the higher mental faculties, new abilities quicken. These include the ability to receive inspirational thoughts and intuitive ideas from a pool which invariably appears in an external form. Telepathy and other mental phenomena are also more likely to appear under conscious control.

It is in such ways that the development of the higher mind refines the mental sheath.

THE CAUSAL FIELD

The causal field is grounded in spiritual reality. It interpenetrates the individual mental field and also rests in the universal field. This energy serves as a bridge between levels of unity and duality. Human experience is invariably dualized into 'me' and 'not me'. In the classic mystical experience there is an overwhelming sense of oneness. The distinction between 'me' and 'not me' simply does not exist.

The world of matter, intertwined with etheric energies, is a plane of effects. What we see about us does not originate upon this level but results from certain laws. The causal level, as its name implies, is a plane of origination, not of manifestation.

The individual human being has little awareness of this level. As we live upon the material plane it would be very difficult for us to maintain this degree of consciousness. Those mystics who have briefly touched this level are often ill-at-ease within the illusions of matter. Nevertheless it is sufficient for us to know that we are rooted into the universal life through the causal field. The causal body is called the anandamaya kosa, or body of bliss.

The subtle energies are just as complicated as the physical form. They respond most readily to applied thought. As in the esoteric saying, 'Energy follows thought,' our subtle energies reflect our mental states for good or ill. The axiom also means that habitual attitudes produce equally engrained patterns of energy, which in turn affect our health and well-being. If we wish to create change we have to take charge of ourselves by changing our patterns of consciousness.

The relationship between the physical and subtle energies is complex. The subtle levels of our being indicate hidden levels of potential within us all. If we each possess seven major centres of awakening, it is certain that the vast majority of us have not yet explored the potential that these represent. Our condition can be likened to a person who sits motionless, having yet to discover the functions of physical limbs. Becoming conscious of our own true nature is difficult and often painful. It will require commitment.

DISCOVERING THE ETHERIC FIELD

Position your hands so that they are facing but not touching each other. You may need to experiment with the distance as there is definitely a critical point at which the energy centres in the palms interact with one another. Begin to move your hands slowly in and out from each other in a bouncing movement. You might already begin to feel something at this point. When the two palm centres interact you will feel what can best be described as a magnetic force between your hands. This is quite different from the experience of general body heat. When you discover this sensation, which cannot be mistaken, you can begin to move the hands slightly further apart. Eventually the contact will be broken as you move beyond the reach of your own energy field.

You can intensify the experience by breathing slowly and rhythmically. On the outbreath visualize white light pouring out from the palms. When you have mastered this exercise you can go on to refine your sensitivity by bouncing the fingertips of one hand off the palm of the other hand. Do this with your eyes closed to develop your other senses. You can also try this with another person. Energy can be sent by one person and received by the other. If you are sending energy your hands will become quite cold; if you are receiving energy you will feel warmth in the localized area. A great deal can be learned from these very simple exercises.

APPROACHING THE GATES

The recent interest in chakra awakening presents us with something of a problem. The West does not have a recognized system for the transmission of this specialized knowledge. In the East, knowledge about the chakras is integrated in the tantric teachings of Tibetan Buddhism and in the Kundalini Yoga of Hinduism. It is firmly based within sacred tradition and within the close bond of the teacher-pupil relationship.

AWAKENING THE CHAKRAS

In *A Treatise on White Magic* by Alice Bailey, the character known as the Tibetan provides us with a working guideline for awakening the chakras. The first essential requirement on the part of a student is character building. This places chakra awakening firmly in the context of daily life and places responsibility directly upon the individual. The Tibetan asks that we examine ourselves to discover the forces that dominate our lives so that we may consciously seek to redress any imbalance. We are asked to 're-organize, re-orientate and rebuild' the very essence of our being. The age-old injunction, 'Know thyself' is still the key to admission into the spiritual life.

The would-be student is therefore asked by the Tibetan to follow the five aspects of Yama, or abstention from evil conduct. These are:

- non-violence
- truthfulness
- sexual continence during certain periods
- non-stealing
- non-greed

The student is also asked to follow the five aspects of Niyama, or virtuous conduct. These are:

- purification
- contentment
- asceticism
- the recitation of sacred sounds
- the worship of divine beings

Yama and Niyama together prepare the mind for enlightenment. This period of re-orientation is considered to be absolutely essential. It is like preparing the ground in readiness for the seed. The Western student could likewise benefit from such a period of preparation.

The Tibetan next asks that we examine our motives for seeking chakra awakening. There has to be a genuine commitment to self-discovery and realization. Anything less will be insufficient to sustain the individual through the inevitable trials and difficulties of the path.

PRACTICAL APPLICATION

After examining our motives for seeking to awaken the chakras, we are asked to examine our commitment to the principle of service. It is important that we should genuinely wish to give the benefits of our awakening for others in some way. Right motivation will naturally lead to a commitment to service. Wrong motivation will create the desire to wield power rather than to offer service. The principle of service is also deeply enshrined within those Western mysteries that uphold the motto, 'To know in order to serve'.

These first three requirements mark a period of preparation and underline the significance of the decision to awaken the centres. By seeking to work with the energies of the chakras we are seeking to discover ourselves. The next three requirements cover the practical application of this commitment. The practice of meditation is recommended to those students who are securely grounded in the stability of the initial requirements.

MEDITATION

Meditation is a primary tool in all areas of spiritual awakening. It was the tenth century sage Goraknath who first commended meditation as a means of activating the chakras in his treatise written in the century. The practitioner uses the many symbols and qualities of the chakras as focal points for meditative practice. Meditation is an essential approach for chakra awakening, which cannot safely take place without the states of mind implicit in meditation.

ABOVE REGULAR MEDITATION IS ESSENTIAL TO ACTIVATE THE CHAKRAS.

29

STUDY

The student is next asked to gain a working knowledge of the centres through intellectual study. This entails gaining an overall under-standing of the names, location, function and inter-relationships between the chakras. According to the Tibetan this will lead naturally to an appreciation of the vibration, colour, tone and astrological significance of the centres.

PRANAYAMA

After the student has created an intellectual framework for personal work, the study of the applied breath, pranayama is recommended as the second practical technique. The subtle energies are highly responsive to controlled breathing, which is quite different from the often shallow and unconscious rhythms of our daily life. Pranayama begins with the development of Yogic breathing. It should take place in a well-ventilated room. It should not be practised on a full stomach or bladder, and the body should be relaxed. Retain the breath as long as is comfortable. Over time, the capacity to hold the breath under control will increase. The classic lotus position is ideal for pranayama practice. However, this posture will be beyond the ability of many Westerners. Instead sit so that the spine is straight.

Yogic Breathing

The Yogic breath is a synthesis of three breaths. It has three parts as air is taken into the abdomen, the chest and then the nasal passages. This is a very calming breath. It also has the power to release tension and bring a sense of wholeness.

1   Inhale deeply.
2   Let the air fill your abdomen. Feel the expansion within your abdomen as the diaphragm stretches.
3   Let the air fill your chest area. Feel your rib cage expand.
4   Let the air move into your throat and nasal passages.
5   On exhalation empty your nasal passages first, then your chest, finally your abdomen.

In this exercise it is important to move the air smoothly and without a break. There should be no separation between inhalation and exhalation.

RIGHT THE SUBTLE ENERGIES ARE RESPONSIVE TO THE CONTROLLED BREATHING PRACTISED IN YOGA.

THE LOCKS

The word bandha means to hold or to tighten. In the locks various parts of the body are gently but firmly contracted. The locks have an effect upon the flow of prana. There are three locks, the neck or chin lock, the diaphragm lock and base lock. These combine breath control with physical control. The bandhas also help release the granthis or psychic knots which impede the flow of prana through the sushumna.

THE NECK LOCK (JALUNDHARA BANDHA)

This lock releases energy blocked in the region of the upper chest. It helps to create space in the upper spine and breaks up locked-in bodily tensions that build up as a result of any concerted mental activity.

1   Sit with a straight back. Place your palms on your knees.
2   Inhale deeply and hold your breath.
3   Bend your head forwards. Pull in your chin and contract your neck. Pull your shoulders up so that your head is resting on the shoulder muscles. Straighten your arms and lock the elbows.
4   Keep your head centred and lock the posture. Retain the breath comfortably. Exhale and release the lock.

Repeat the lock three times.

31

THE DIAPHRAGM LOCK (UDDIYANA BANDHA)

This lock stimulates the solar plexus chakra. As this is the distribution centre for prana throughout the body this lock improves the spread of prana generally.

1   Sit with a straight back. Place your palms on your knees.
2   Exhale deeply, emptying your abdomen and chest.
3   Lift your diaphragm. Pull the organs of the upper abdomen up and back towards your spine.
4   Lock the posture. Hold while it is comfortable.
    Release and inhale.

THE ROOT LOCK (MULABANDHA)

This is the most complex of the locks. It has a powerful effect on the energies at the base of the spine. It can also release creative energies.

1   Sit with a straight back. Place your hands on your knees.
2   Exhale deeply. Contract the muscles of your perineum and draw them upwards.
3   Draw in the lower abdomen towards the spine.
4   Hold the lock while it is comfortable. Release and inhale. Repeat.

The breath is a profound tool for creating physical, emotional and intellectual change. The breathing pattern mirrors the way in which the individual interacts with the world and with himself or herself. It is frequently shallow and incomplete. The traditional breathing patterns, including alternate nostril breathing, hara breathing and the breath of fire can have dynamic effects. These exercises work upon the physical body by increasing the supply of oxygen – which assists the detoxification process– and have a direct effect upon the energies of the subtle fields.

ALTERNATE NOSTRIL BREATHING

Stage 1

1   Sit straight with your hands on your knees. Place your right hand on your forehead and place your middle and index fingers between your eyebrows. The thumb is placed by the right nostril and the ring finger is placed by the left nostril.
2   Close your right nostril with the thumb.
3   Inhale, then exhale through the left nostril five times.
4   Release your right nostril and press your left nostril with the ring finger. Inhale, then exhale through the right nostril five times.

This completes one cycle. Practise until 25 cycles can be performed.

Stage 2

1   Close the right nostril with your thumb and inhale through the left.

2   After inhalation, close the left nostril, release the right nostril and exhale out through it.

3   Inhale through the right nostril and close it at the end of the inhalation. Open the left nostril and exhale.

This completes one cycle. The lengths of the inhalation and exhalation should be equal.

Stage 3

1   Close your right nostril and inhale through the left.
    At the end of the inhalation, close both nostrils and retain the breath.

2   Exhale through your right nostril and then inhale through it keeping your left nostril closed.

3   Close both nostrils and retain the breath.

4   Open your left nostril and exhale through it.

This completes one cycle. Each action: inhalation, retention and exhalation, should be performed to the count of five. Practise until 25 cycles can be performed.

Refinements of this exercise later include altering the ratio between times of inhalation, retention and exhalation to produce a final ratio of 1:8:6. This exercise is worth the hard work that is required to master it. Each stage should be practised over a period of months

LEFT ALTERNATE NOSTRIL BREATHING CLEARS THE NADIS AND INCREASES THE SUPPLY OF OXYGEN TO THE BLOOD, THUS WORKING DIRECTLY ON THE SUBTLE ENERGIES.

until the procedure has been completely integrated. This practice clears the nadis, brings calmness of mind and increases the supply of oxygen to the blood. It brings awareness of the hot and cold solar and lunar currents carried by the breath.

THE BELLOWS BREATH OR BREATH OF FIRE

1   Sit straight with hands on your knees.
2   Place the right hand on the forehead with the middle fingers between the eyes. Place your thumb beside the right nostril and your ring finger beside the left nostril.
3   Close the right nostril with your thumb. Breathe rapidly and rhythmically through the left nostril 20 times, expanding and contracting the abdomen.
4   Close both nostrils and perform mulabanda or jalandhara.
5   Close the left nostril and breathe 20 times with quick but rhythmical expansions and contractions of the abdomen.
6   Inhale, close both nostrils and perform jalandhara or mulabanda. This completes one cycle. Perform three cycles.

The bellows breath clears the lungs. It stimulates the appetite and digestion. This is a powerful technique for awakening Kundalini. It should not be practised by people with high blood pressure or heart conditions. It should not be done on a full stomach. This is a vigorous exercise and you may feel a surge of pranic energy shooting up the spine. This may make you feel a little light-headed but there should be no feelings of faintness or excessive giddiness.

PSYCHIC BREATHING

By contrast, this is a very quiet and gentle breath. It may be practised for long periods in conjunction with meditation techniques. It produces a calming effect on the nervous system.

1   Close the glottis at the back of your throat.
2   Breathe deeply and softly. You will find that this produces a slight snoring sound.

The combination of mind control and breath control should make it increasingly possible to direct prana throughout the body or even outside the body where it can be used to heal another person. Sensitivity to prana will increase with practice. It can be experienced as a sensation of movement or through a sudden change in localized body temperature. The inner eye will also become attuned to the flow of prana which appears to the mind's eye as flecks of brightness, shining filaments of white light, or showers of sparks. Techniques which combine breath control and visualization help this process considerably.

CIRCULATION OF LIGHT

1   Sit with a straight spine.
2   Imagine a reservoir or pool of light at the base of your spine.
3   Inhale slowly and deeply (use the psychic breath). As you do so draw energy in the form of light up from the base chakra. Let it rise up through the sushumna to the top of your head. When it reaches the top of the head see a cascade of light fountaining out through the head.
4   Let this light circulate on either side of your body and be drawn in again at the base chakra.

This completes one cycle. Perform five cycles.

THE INNER SPIRALS

These exercises develop the awareness of the psychic pathways between the muladhara and the ajna centres.

1   Sit straight with hands on your knees.
2   Become aware of the muladhara chakra at the base of your spine.
3   See the pranic channel starting at the right of the chakra. See it curving out towards the right of the body before it curves back to the left to cross the sushumna at the svadisthana chakia.
4   It emerges on the left side of the body from the mid-line and curves back to cross the sushumna at the solar plexus chakra.
5   It emerges on the right side of the body to curve back to the left

before it sweeps back to pass at the heart centre.

6   It emerges on the left and then swings back to cross the
    sushumna to pass beneath at the throat chakra.

7   It emerges on the right of centre from where it flows into the
    ajna chakra at the centre point on the sushumna.

The prana will descend via the alternative spiral route.

1   Visualize the ajna chakra between your eyebrows.
    See the pranic current starting at the right side just above
    your right nostril.

2   See this channel flowing out over the right cheek. It then turns
    leftwards before it crosses the sushumna at the mid-line and
    passes at the throat chakra.

3   It emerges from the mid-line moving towards the left before it
    curves back towards the right and crosses the mid-line at the
    sushumna passing at the heart chakra.

4   It emerges to the right side of the body, then curves back to the
    mid-line crossing the sushumna at the solar plexus chakra.

5   It emerges towards the left side of the body, and curves back to
    cross the sushumna at the sacral chakra.

6   It emerges to the right before curving again to cross the
    sushumna at the base chakra.

7   It emerges upon the left and then curves to the right to enter the
    base chakra.

As this is quite a difficult exercise, you might find it easier to
break it into at least two parts.

These exercises need to be repeated over and over again to to make
real progress. Some people are able to see and move prana very
rapidly, but others will find it a slower process requiring patience.
The traditional methods for awakening the subtle energies – breath
control, meditation and physical postures – constitute an integrated
approach to working with the centres. No serious student can expect
to avoid any of these disciplines.

AWAKENING THE CHAKRAS
THROUGH YOGA

Yoga offers a thoroughly integrated system for awakening the chakras. With Yoga, the initial period of preparation is followed by gradual absorption of the techniques of pranayama, meditation and physical asanas or postures. The postures function at many levels. They have an obvious effect upon physical well-being by releasing muscle tension, strengthening internal systems and releasing stiffness in the joints. The asanas also have an impact upon the etheric levels by working upon the nadis, which circulate the subtle energies. When combined with certain states of mind, Yoga also affects the astral and mental levels of being by bringing calmness and control.

Hiroshi Motoyama has allocated a series of postures specifically to the chakras. These are organized into two groups. The first group serves as preparatory postures which increase the absorption of prana into the body and regulate the flow. The second group strengthens the sushumna and facilitates the flow of prana through this vital nadi. Those who wish to work with these postures will find thorough explanations in books such as *Light on Yoga* by B K S Iyengar.

37

RIGHT THE PHYSICAL POSTURES OF YOGA
ARE NOT ONLY BENEFICIAL TO THE BODY
BUT CAN ALSO HELP TO CIRCULATE
THE SUBTLE ENERGIES AND THUS
AWAKEN THE CHAKRAS.

ASANAS FOR PROMOTING PRANA CIRCULATION

(Reproduced with kind permission from The Theosophical Publishing House.)

1 Lie flat on your back with your arms at your sides, palms upwards; enter a relaxed state. This is the shavasana (Corpse pose).

2 When relaxed and ready sit on the floor with legs extended. Place your hands palms-down on the floor beside your hips and lean slightly backwards. Flex your toes ten times; flex your ankles ten times back and forth; then draw circles in both directions with each of your feet.

3 Place your right ankle on your left thigh. Hold your ankle with your right hand, rotate your foot ten times in each direction. Repeat with your left foot on your right thigh.

4 Raise your right knee and bend it. Clasp your hands under your thigh. Straighten your leg without touching the ground. Repeat ten times with each leg.

5 Place your right foot on your left thigh. Hold your left knee with your left hand and place your right hand on top of your bent knee. Gently move the bent leg up and down. Repeat with the other leg.

6 Place the soles of your feet together and bring the heels as close to your body as possible. Allow the knees to drop as far as they are able.

7 Squat on the floor. Place your palms on your knees and walk while keeping the squatting position.

8 Sit in the original position. Extend your arms forward at shoulder height. Clench and unclench the fingers of each hand ten times. Keep your arms extended forwards. Bend your hands back up as far as possible, then down. Repeat ten times.

9 Extend your arms forward. Drop one arm. Make a fist with your other hand. Rotate your wrists ten times in each direction.

10 Extend your arms forward palms up. Bend both your arms at the

elbows and touch your shoulders with your finger tips. Repeat ten times. Then repeat with your arms extended to the sides.

11 Touch your shoulders with your fingertips. Move your elbows in circles in each direction ten times.

These exercises stimulate the joints and help to keep prana freely circulating. Source points of energy are located near the wrists and ankles. These are related to specific organs. Using these joints will keep energy flowing. The terminal points for the major meridians are located in the fingers and toes. This group of asanas is simple, yet very invigorating.

THE SUSHUMNA

These asanas work especially on the spine. They bring strength and suppleness with practice. Instructions on these postures will be found in most books on Yoga.

1 The Mountain Pose (Tadasana).

2 Hasta Uttanasana.

3 Pada Hastasana.

4 Yoga Mudra pose (Yogasana).

5 The Pincers pose (Paschimottanasana).

6 Pada prasarita paschimottanasana.

7 The Cobra pose (Bhujangasana). Concentrate on the vishuddi chakra.

8 The Bow pose (Dhanurasana). Concentrate on the vishuddi chakra.

9 The Plough (Halasana). Concentrate on the vishuddi chakra.

10 The Fish pose (Matsyasana). Concentrate on the manipura or anahata chakra.

11 The Triangle (Trikonasana).

12 Dynamic Spinal Twist.

13 Half Spinal Twist (Arda matsyendrasana). Concentrate on the ajna chakra.

14 Spinal Twist Prostration pose (Bhu Namanasana).

Chakra Dowsing

It is possible to assess the state of individual chakras by dowsing with a pendulum. Dowsing can be thought of as a means of amplifying a response that is normally below the threshold of consciousness. We are unconsciously able to relate to many different vibrations generated by varying forms. Organic life, plants, minerals and animate beings all generate energy fields that extend beyond the physical structure. Dowsing is a skill that is best acquired through experience. It is the easiest thing in the world to construct a pendulum from a ring and a length of thread, suspend it over a variety of objects and observe your own deep reaction to the energy system magnified by the pendulum. Experienced dowsers might like to try chakra dowsing for themselves. It is best if the person having a chakra reading lies down flat on their back. The person dowsing can kneel beside them. The pendulum should be suspended over the general area of the chakra,

40

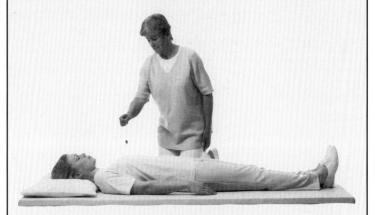

ABOVE THE WAY IN WHICH THE LOWERED PENDULUM ROTATES CAN REVEAL THE STATE OF THE SUBJECT'S CHAKRAS TO AN EXPERIENCED DOWSER.

and slowly lowered until it connects with the energy field of the individual. This will vary from person to person. When the pendulum connects with the chakra it will begin to rotate in either a clockwise or an anti-clockwise direction. It will describe a circle, which seems to indicate the circumference of the chakra itself. The speed of rotation is also indicative of the activity of the chakra. The pendulum can be sluggish on occasion or surprisingly rapid. Circular rotation in either direction is indicative of activity and vitality within the chakra. It is more common to find chakras that rotate in a clockwise direction. Physical illness, mirrored within the activity of the relevant chakra, produces either a linear movement of the pendulum or even produces no activity at all, which means the chakra has closed for a while. Dowsing in this way can be illuminating. It shows us very clearly the nature of the relationship between the physical and the etheric levels.

CHAKRAS AND HEALTH

The chakras are excellent indicators of well-being. When a chakra is blocked or closed the individual is no longer able to access the corresponding energies. The relationship between the physical and supra-physical energies is reciprocal and circular. Imbalance at one level is reflected by imbalance at another. We can therefore use the chakras as a means of diagnosis.

The body operates as a hologram, the whole being reflected in the parts. The therapeutic disciplines of acupuncture, reflexology and massage each demonstrates the principle that the body mirrors wholeness within its parts. We can therefore locate points in the hands and feet that correspond to the chakras. The reflex points for

AFFIRMATIONS

Chakras are highly sensitive to deliberate thought patterns. Affirmations for each chakra are a good way of keeping intentions focused as we go about daily life.

Create your own affirmations based on these suggestions. Let your affirmation be simple and let it be positive. The affirmation should summarize what the chakra means for you. These positive self-created affirmations can act as a powerful antidote to the endless negative affirmations projected upon us by adults and authority figures as we grow up. How much better to affirm that 'I have the freedom to create my own reality,' than constantly to be told, 'You can't do that.' The affirmation can be used like a meditation while you are working with one chakra. It can be repeated aloud or used silently. It is also a good idea to write down the affirmation and take it with you wherever you go. This simple act merely serves to remind you of its value. The affirmation is best used in conjunction with a dynamic approach.

CHAKRA	AFFIRMATION
Muladhara	I am a part of the living universe. I acknowledge my connections with all living beings.
Svadisthana	I have the power to create. I am able to bring something new into this life.
Manipura	I am in control of my own power. I am able to make my own decisions.
Anahata	I feel compassion for all living beings.
Vishuddha	I express my deepest thoughts and feelings with clarity.
Ajna	I am in tune with an infinite source of guidance.
Sahasrara	I am that I am.

the pituitary gland assigned to the brow chakra are located on the thumbs and big toes for example. A skilled practitioner can use these points both for diagnosis and as part of treatment.

Working with energy meridians or nodal points requires training and skill if it is to be successful. Muscle testing provides the basis for all touch for health techniques. The relative strengths of the chakras can also be assessed in this way. It is very easy to do and gives a rough and ready assessment. The test requires two people, the testee and the tester. The testee stands with right arm outstretched with palm down; the left hand is placed over the chakras one at a time. The tester applies a firm downwards pressure to the outstretched arm. The testee is asked to resist as each of the chakras is tested in turn. This test is most interesting. It is impossible to cheat for, try as you might, if a chakra is weak you will not be able to hold out against the pressure from your friend.

There is an even simpler version of this test. The testee connects the tip of the right index finger to the tip of the right thumb. The left hand is placed over the chakras one at a time. The tester tries to pull the testee's thumb and finger apart. It is especially helpful to apply a test to assess the strength of a chakra when you are unwell. There is a great deal to be learned at an individual level by matching patterns of physical illness with patterns of etheric disturbance. You can learn to detect the point of recovery, when the energies flow normally through the related chakra. This point often precedes physical recovery.

BACH FLOWER REMEDIES

The chakras are also highly responsive to approaches, such as the Bach flower remedies, that work specifically upon the subtle energies. The right remedy can have an extraordinarily liberating effect upon a blocked chakra. As the Bach flower remedies are quite harmless it is safe to experiment with them in conjunction with chakra work, and they also work very well when used in conjunction with other intensive approaches.

LEFT DEPENDING ON WHICH CHAKRA IS BLOCKED, YOU CAN CHOOSE A SPECIFIC BACH FLOWER REMEDY TO WORK ON IT.

DREAMS AND CHAKRAS

Deliberate work upon a chakra usually has an impact. Sometimes it is obvious, especially if the individual concerned is sensitive and the results are overt. At other times progress seems slow and the results appear in diffuse forms, new attitudes and new levels of awareness. Chakra work often produces highly symbolic and charged dreams which reveal the condition of the relevant chakra.

Dreaming itself can be used as a vehicle for chakra work if the individual is sufficiently attuned to their own dream processes. Dream work can be used as part of an overall strategy for chakra awakening. If you wish to incubate a dream you will need to spend the time before sleeping immersed in the relevant images and thoughts. You will also need to develop the ability to recall your dream images as you wake.

ABOVE WORKING ON YOUR CHAKRAS CAN PRODUCE HIGHLY SYMBOLIC DREAMS.

CREATING IMAGES OF CHAKRAS

One of the simplest and most illuminating ways of connecting with the chakras is simply to allow the inner mind to provide symbols and images for each of the chakras. Prepare by assembling a wide range of colours in any medium that you wish. Take a large sheet of paper and enter a quiet meditative state. Attune yourself to each of the chakras in turn and simply draw the images that come to mind. This exercise is quite fascinating. Dark, sombre colours inevitably reveal the inability to express the energy of a particular chakra. Organic shapes and flowing lines indicate harmony and ease of expression. Integration or separation reveals itself in the form and degree of connections between the chakras. The relative size of individual chakras and their emphasis in the whole pattern reveals the degree of spontaneous use.

Having some measure of the overall interaction of the chakras at any given moment is important as we begin to operate more consciously with the energies. We might like to work on a chakra that feels blocked and inaccessible. We might like to work with a physical symptom by engaging the energy that underpins it. We might simply like to have some way of observing the effects of our conscious interaction with chakra energy. Experiment with the approaches suggested, develop a way that comes naturally to you and make it part of your life. There is one golden rule, however, when it comes to work of this nature. If you experience dramatic results that make you feel unstable or off-balance, stop! Do not apply any further pressure. Try to rest and allow the energies to stabilize. This is especially important if you are working on your own. In mystery tradition it is said, 'Make haste slowly.'

45

THE KEYS TO THE CHAKRAS

CHAPTER THREE

If a picture is worth a thousand words then a symbolic picture is worth words beyond number. A symbol is open ended; it expands the mind and allows ideas to roam, to free associate, and to gel into newly formed patterns. Universal symbols retain power across the centuries. Undiminished by the passing of time and undimmed by changing values, these symbols have the capacity to awaken each new generation. Words are often restrictive. I can pass information to you through words. I can tell you about the chakras. Yet words alone will not initiate you into the inner meaning of the chakras. You are the only person able to do this by inwardly absorbing the attributes, qualities and functions of the chakras through meditation and active participation.

CHAKRA CORRESPONDENCES

Each of the chakras is symbolically described using a system of correspondences. The chakras are allocated to colours, geometric shapes (yantras), elements, presiding deities, animal symbols and sounds (mantras). Each chakra is also described as having a particular number of petals. These have been said to represent the vibration of each chakra. Others have suggested that these numbers refer to the spinal nerves related to each plexus. The Tibetan tells us that the word 'petal' only symbolizes an expression of force. Sanskrit letters are also allocated to each of the chakras.

These symbolic descriptions can be thought of as a shorthand or code that summarizes the essential qualities of the chakra. A symbol can be thought of as a door. It remains tightly shut unless you have the right key.

The chakra images convey little if you just look at them. You need to internalize the forms through meditation. Then the door will swing open easily. You will understand not merely the appearance but the meaning of each of the symbolic representations.

COLOURS

Traditionally, each of the chakras is assigned a colour of the rainbow: red, orange, yellow, green, blue, indigo and violet. This does not mean that the chakras themselves are these colours. The colours indicate the relative vibration of the chakras, moving from the slowest at the base to the most rapid at the top of the head. The colours themselves also carry certain symbolic values which the Western mind easily comprehends. Red is strong and forceful; orange is less aggressive but nevertheless fiery; yellow is solar and warming; green is cool and promotes natural growth; blue is the colour of healing; indigo is expansive; violet is associated with spiritual aspiration.

47

YANTRAS

The traditional chakra images are also coloured according to a specific code indicated in the *Sat-Cakra-Nirupana*. The colour of the petals, the letters inscribed on them and the yantra

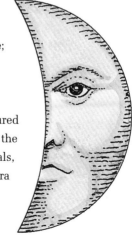

RIGHT THE CRESCENT MOON IS THE YANTRA FOR THE SACRAL CHAKRA.

attributed to each chakra, are all assigned to specific colours. These also carry symbolic values. The yellow square of privithi, the yantra of the base chakra, signifies elemental earth. The crescent moon, yantra of the sacral chakra, is white signifying elemental water. The triangle, yantra of the solar plexus chakra, is red signifying elemental fire. The hexagon of the heart chakra is a smoky green, signifying the element of air. The circular yantra of the vishuddi chakra is again white. The ajna chakra is predominantly white. It does not have a yantra. This colour is associated with the coolness of the moon and Nirvana. The Sahasrara is not described either in terms of colour or a yantra.

THE CHAKRAS: COLOURS

CHAKRA	PETALS	LETTERS	YANTRA
Base	Crimson	Gold	Yellow
Sacral	Vermilion	Lightning	White
Solar Plexus	Blue-green	Blue	Red
Heart	Vermilion	Vermilion	Smoky
Throat	Smoky purple	Red	White
Brow	White	White	White

ELEMENTS

Each of the chakras is also assigned to an element. This links the qualities of the chakra to a constellation of ideas which are represented by the elemental qualities.

- The element of earth, attributed to the base chakra, does not refer solely to physical earth. It refers to the qualities of being that might also be thought of as earthy in themselves: practicality, survival, organization and structure. Earth is slow to change, it has to be manipulated. It is fertile but requires labour; it is our provider and mother.

- The element of water, attributed to the sacral chakra, refers to qualities that could be said to be of a watery nature: reflection, movement, flow and depth. Water has no shape of its own; it is passive in relation to its surroundings. It cleanses and revives. Our bodies contain and require water; life begins in the womb. The menstrual cycle is closely connected to the lunar cycle. There is a close connection between all waters and the influence of the moon.

- The element of fire is assigned to the solar plexus chakra. It includes those qualities that might be thought fiery: action, change, expansion and passion. Fire is difficult to confine. It is expansive and volatile. It warms and comforts. Metabolic change generates warmth. When our stomachs are empty we are cold. Fire has the power to change things from one state to another. Fire is always active but it needs constantly to be fuelled.

- Elemental air, attributed to the heart chakra, refers to those qualities that might be termed airy by nature: pervasion, omnipresence and invisibility. Air cannot be seen; we cannot touch air yet it touches us; it can be seen only through its effect. Winds circulate around our planet in huge patterns affecting us all. Air is never still; it is active. It is unlimited and shared by everyone.

49

THE CHAKRAS: THE ELEMENTS

CHAKRA	ELEMENT
Base	Earth
Sacral	Water
Solar Plexus	Fire
Heart	Air
Throat	Akasa
Brow	None
Crown	None

- This element of akasa is attributed to the throat chakra. It is also called ether or spirit and refers to the eternal undying qualities that underlie all manifest forms. Its outer form might be thought of as prana, the universal life force. Akasa is beyond both space and time. It represents a mystery.

Neither the brow nor crown chakras are attributed to any particular elements by tradition. Anodea Judith, writing in *Wheels of Life*, attributes light to the brow chakra and thought to the crown chakra. The elemental attributions are best comprehended through meditation.

DEITIES

Each of the chakras is assigned to a ruling deity or pair of deities. These figures act as initiators into the essential experience of the chakra. The deities are often depicted with many heads and arms to indicate their various qualities or aspects. The god-forms hold items that symbolize the lessons that the chakra holds for the aspirant. These symbols can be used as focal points in meditation. When the student has an understanding of these symbols, the deities can be visualized holding all the various items.

The dual rulership of each chakra, except in the case of the brow chakra, is especially interesting. The chakras are constantly moderating yin and yang energies. The point of balance is personified by the male and female deities. The deity representing the ajna (brow) chakra is androgynous: both male and female. It is at this point that

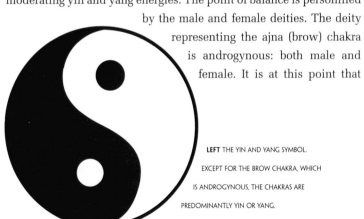

LEFT THE YIN AND YANG SYMBOL. EXCEPT FOR THE BROW CHAKRA, WHICH IS ANDROGYNOUS, THE CHAKRAS ARE PREDOMINANTLY YIN OR YANG.

THE CHAKRAS: PRESIDING DEITIES

CHAKRA	DEITIES
Base	Brahma holding staff, gourd, rosary.
	Dakini holding spear, staff with skull atop, sword, cup.
Sacral	Vishnu holding conch shell, disc, war club, lotus.
	Rakini holding trident, lotus, drum, battle axe.
Solar Plexus	Rudra holding rosary, fire weapon.
	Lakini holding thunderbolt, fire weapon.
Heart	Isa holds nothing. Kakini holding noose, skull.
Throat	Sadasiva holding noose, goad, serpent, trident, fire weapon, vajra, sword, battle axe, sword, bell. Gauri holding noose, goad, arrow, bow.
Brow	Sakti Hakini holding book, drum, staff with skull, rosary.

51

the ida and pingala currents merge with sushumna to create one current that is neither yin nor yang.

The deities make two gestures, the abhayamudra to dispel fears and the varada to grant boons. If the chakra is approached in the right spirit there is nothing to fear. If you wish to work with the Eastern deities you will need to study the relevant mythologies and understand the forces they represent, and you will need to be able to visualize their forms clearly. If you are unable to do this, visualize a pair of rulers for each chakra, perhaps as lord and lady or even as king and queen. Use an androgynous figure for the ajna chakra.

Visualization is not an exercise in mental skill. It is the creation of an appropriate vehicle, a thought form. The act of visualizing draws upon the faculties of the right hemisphere of the brain, which also provides the ability to understand symbolic forms. Drawing upon this hemisphere also calls into play emotional depths that remain untapped by sheer rationalization. Building a god-form in the mind's eye should elicit an emotional reaction. If it does not, the exercise is not being performed to the fullest. The Tibetan tradition includes highly complex and detailed visualization of deities. These are invariably dissolved into emptiness at the termination of the practice.

ANIMAL SYMBOLS

The functions of the chakras are additionally symbolized by various animals. These are the elephant with seven trunks, the makara – a crocodile-like creature – the ram and the antelope. These also have mythological connections with certain deities. The elephant with seven trunks is Airavata, the elephant of Indra. At the base chakra Airavata wears a black collar to indicate that he is bound to the forces of ignorance. This chakra is assigned to the element of earth. The elephant reappears without the restrictive black noose as the symbol for the throat chakra. The elephant is now pure white indicating freedom from ignorance. The makara, symbol of the svadisthana chakra (assigned to water), is the emblem of Varuna, lord of the seas. The ram found at the solar plexus chakra (assigned to fire) is the companion to Agni, the god of fire. The gazelle or antelope, found at the heart chakra (assigned to air) is the vehicle of Vayu god of the winds. These animal symbols underline the elemental correspondences and also carry the mantra for each chakra.

MANTRAS

The mantra is a sounded meditation that resonates with the vibration of the chakra. Each chakra is assigned to a different bija mantra or seed syllable. Starting at the base chakra the bija mantras are Lam, Vam, Ram, Yam, Ham and Om. There is no bija mantra for the crown chakra. Each of these seed sounds is depicted within the centre of the lotus. The *Sat-Cakra-Nirupana* describes these mantras

as being seated upon the back of the appropriate animal. The mantra rides upon the animal, set within the yantra, watched by the deities bearing symbolic gifts. These are all held within the circle, set about with petals inscribed with Sanskrit letters.

LEFT THE SYMBOL FOR 'OM', THE MANTRA FOR THE BROW CHAKRA.

Here are the keys to the chakras, they await you.

THE GATEWAY
OF EARTH

Our journey begins here at the base chakra. The Sanskrit name for this chakra is muladhara. It is drawn from two words meaning 'root' and 'base' or 'support'. This aptly describes the function of this centre, namely to provide a powerful anchor that links us with all living things. It is our base in the physical world. We too are part of nature. We share many functions and instincts with other living creatures; we are all part of one world. If we fail to acknowledge such things we are simply deluded. This sense of belonging within the physical world is vital in our dealings with it. If we believe ourselves to be separate from the natural world as outsiders, observers and manipulators we make a grave error. The base chakra primarily represents the will to survive, the fundamental drive itself. Without this drive there is no willingness to battle against adverse circumstances or to adapt to new situations.

FUNCTIONS OF THE BASE CHAKRA

The base chakra, unlike the others, faces downwards towards the earth where it picks up and transmits subtle geodetic forces. Such contact is dependent upon proximity to the physical earth. The

THE BASE CHAKRA: TABLE OF CORRESPONDENCES

LOCATION: Perineum, between the anus and the genitals

SANSKRIT NAME: Muladhara, derived from mula meaning 'root' and 'adhara' meaning base or support

FUNCTION: Survival, grounding

ELEMENT: Earth

INNER STATE: Stability

GLANDS: Adrenals

BODY PARTS: Legs, feet, bones, large intestine

MALFUNCTION: Obesity, haemorrhoids, constipation, sciatica

COLOUR: Red

SEED SOUND: Lam

SENSE: Smell

VOWEL SOUND: O as in rope

PETALS: Four: vam, śaṃ, ṣaṃ, saṃ

ANIMAL SYMBOLS: Bull, elephant, ox

DEITIES: Brahma, Dakini, Gaia, Demeter, Persephone, Erishkagel, Ana, Ceres, Ceridwen, Geb, Hades, Pwyll

RIGHT THE BULL IS ONE OF THE ANIMAL SYMBOLS FOR THE BASE CHAKRA.

trappings of civilization can insulate us totally unless we make a conscious effort to counterbalance this effect. Walking in an open place is not just good exercise, it is a good opportunity to connect with the earth beneath our feet.

LEFT THE ELEMENT OF EARTH CORRESPONDS TO THE PHYSICAL NATURE OF THE BASE CHAKRA.

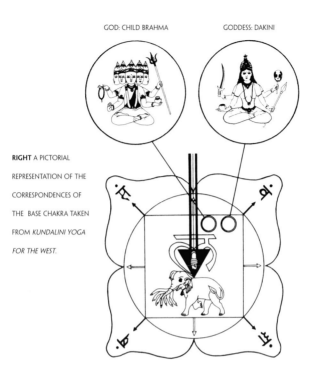

GOD: CHILD BRAHMA   GODDESS: DAKINI

RIGHT A PICTORIAL REPRESENTATION OF THE CORRESPONDENCES OF THE BASE CHAKRA TAKEN FROM *KUNDALINI YOGA FOR THE WEST*.

56

The colour red is attributed to this chakra. It is the colour of life blood. Red ochre was frequently smeared on the bodies of the dead to represent rebirth into a new life. It has come to symbolize the passions and the life force itself. The colour has passed into common usage in the language: when we are angry we see red; if we paint the town red, we indulge in extravagant and boisterous behaviour. The colour red is assigned to the planet Mars, which symbolizes dynamic, energetic and even aggressive forces. The colour red exhibits the lowest frequency in the colour spectrum. It corresponds well to the qualities and functions of the base chakra.

The base chakra is well named. It represents our most primitive instincts and drives. It is not surprising that the glands associated with this chakra are the adrenals, which are responsible for the fight or flight response through the output of adrenalin. This is a primitive response, a leftover from those distant days when our ancestors had to run or fight for their lives. We like to think of ourselves as being civilized and sophisticated, but in dire situations we can find ourselves battling for daily survival, as did our forefathers.

WHEN IT IS BLOCKED

In the body, this chakra rules the legs and feet, the bones and the large intestines. Imbalances at this level can bring about obesity, sciatica, haemorrhoids, constipation and, in men, prostate problems. Individuals with these difficulties would benefit from working with the energies of the base chakra. Imbalances at this level can also create psychological problems such as conditions of grief, depression and instability. These reflect darkened views of the world. Self-indulgent behaviour such as greed, avarice and extreme self-centredness, which each represent limited views about the self, can also result from blockages at this level. Over-identification with this state of consciousness brings an excessive concern for material stability and external values such as status, power and prestige. The restricted outlook then becomes self-perpetuating. It is not difficult to see this kind of consciousness in the world at large.

WHEN IT IS ACTIVE

The base chakra houses karmic forces. Chakras hold information and memory like computer disks constantly updating the amount of life data on file. The contents of each chakra remain undisclosed until the appropriate 'key' is recognized. This key can take many forms, for example applied energy, meditation or physical stimulus. A sudden awakening can unexpectedly tap distant memory and release repressed emotions in a volcanic way.

When the base chakra is active and balanced there is a sense of purpose, a sense of belonging to the natural world and a willingness to take personal responsibility for actions and deeds.

ORIENTATION EXERCISES

1   Choose an earth deity. Study their mythology and familiarize
    yourself with the forms in which they have been represented.
2   Explore your own relationship with the natural world by
    considering: What does the earth give you and what do you give
    the earth?
3   Meditate on the element of earth.

ASANAS

BODY DROPS

This exercise works on governor vessel 1, the acupuncture point at
the base of the spine.

1   Sit on the floor with legs stretched out in front of you.
2   Support yourself by placing your hands on the floor behind you.
3   Arch your buttocks and bounce gently on the base of the spine.

LEG STRETCHES

This exercise stretches the sciatic nerve, the body's largest nerve.

1   Sit on the floor with legs outstretched in front of you.
2   Lift upwards in the spine.
3   Bend your right knee and place the heel between the genitals
    and rectum, so that you are sitting on the heel. This stimulates
    conception vessel 1. Your left leg
    remains straight out in

RIGHT THE LEG STRETCH, PERFORMED
WHILST SITTING ON ONE HEELS, STRETCH
THE SCIATIC NERVE AND STIMULATES
CONCEPTION VESSEL 1.

front.

4   Reach forward and take hold of your leg at the shin, ankle or even the foot if this is comfortable.

5   Exhale and bend forwards, bring your head towards the left knee, but do not slump the spine forwards.

6   Repeat by working on the other side of the body.

SITTING ON THE HEELS (VAJRASANA)

Sitting in Vajrasana stimulates the urinary meridian, which runs down the back of the legs. Concentrating on the nose stimulates the muladhara by focusing on the point where ida and pingala terminate. Concentrating the perineum focuses awareness on the area where ida and pingala originate.

1   Sit on the heels with the knees pointing forwards and kept slightly apart.

2   Place the hands on the legs, with the wrists resting lightly on the thighs.

3   Close the eyes and direct the attention to the tip of your nose for several minutes as a meditation.

4   Shift the attention to the perineum for several minutes as a meditation. The perineum can also be contracted and relaxed sequentially.

RIGHT MEDITATING IN THE VAJRASANA POSTURE
HELPS TO STIMULATE THE URINARY MERIDIAN.

59

VISUALIZATION: THE FOUR HORIZONS

See before you a circle traced out upon the ground. See the four directions marked clearly on it. In the centre of the circle stands a figure wearing a dark robe of coarse cloth with a hood. This is your chosen earth deity. As you watch, the figure invites you to stand in the centre of the circle. You stand together at the centre. The figure draws a small rod from the folds of the cloak and points towards the distant eastern horizon.

You find yourself watching a group of men hunting together on foot armed only with spears and sticks. Now you run beside them as they pursue a great animal ahead. They surround the great beast, which towers over them. They work together, attacking and wounding the giant creature to bring it down. You feel something of their experience: terror mingled with excitement, exuberance combined with concentration. You feel a flush of adrenalin. As the beast is brought down, your legs seem to give way as if you too had participated in the chase and the kill.

The scene fades and you return to the centre of the circle. The figure directs your attention towards the next horizon. Now you find yourself amidst great clouds of dust and the sound of the clash of arms. You are in the thick of battle. Two armies are pitting themselves one against the other, without mercy. You wonder why they have taken to arms. You hear the sound of horses in pain and the distant cries of men cut and dying on the ground. You do not wait to see the outcome of the day for you cannot know if the victor has a just cause. You can only see the slaughter of men and hear the sounds of battle. You turn away. The scene fades and you return to the central point.

Your guide directs your attention to the next quarter. Find yourself standing at a city gate. A steep cobbled street rises ahead. On either side of the street people lie, or sit hunched up, motionless. Ragged children hang on to emaciated women. At the top of the rise the street opens out onto a square, which is decorated with flags and regalia. Yet in the doorways and corners around the square you can still see the ragged figures. Into the square comes a great procession: soldiers, musicians and dancers all in extravagant costumes. Now come the rulers of the city, carried aloft in decorated palanquins by men. They pass in a blaze of colour. You turn away. The scene fades. You are back at the central point again.

TIPS FOR WORKING WITH THE BASE CHAKRA

DREAM IMAGES

Work on the base chakra can spontaneously produce a wide range of images, indicating that an awakening has taken place, for example dreams that take place underground and reveal a hitherto untapped source of power, possibly in a subterranean chamber, basement or cellar; dreams of underground fire; dreams of opening a hidden trap door; dreams that feature digging for hidden treasure or unearthing items of significance. Dreams featuring a serpent, bull, elephant or other massive beast also relate to this level of consciousness.

BACH FLOWER REMEDIES

Cherry plum	6	Learning to let go
Clematis	9	Grounding
Gorse	13	Integration of joy and sorrow
Pine	24	Taking responsibility for your own life
Sweet chestnut	30	Trusting your own development

LEFT THE SWEET CHESTNUT
BACH FLOWER REMEDY CAN
HELP YOU TO TRUST IN YOUR
OWN DEVELOPMENT.

MUSIC

This chakra responds to earthy tribal music and primitive natural rhythms. Try to work on the base chakra by listening to the authentic sounds of drumming or chanting, which may encourage you to dance, stamp your feet or jump.

Your guide directs your attention to the last quarter. You find yourself transported to a small hillside overlooking a paddy field. In the field a group of women are at work planting rice. They are bent over as they work. You watch them as they work, slowly, patiently, methodically moving through the field in a subtle rhythm of work. You hope that their harvest will be a good one. The whole community depends upon it. The scene fades from view and you find yourself standing at the central point once more.

Beside you is the figure of your chosen deity. The figure turns to you and speaks: 'You have watched others; how will you use the powers of earth?' Take time to reflect. The scene finally fades.

THE GATEWAY
OF THE MOON

CHAPTER FIVE

Rising up from the base chakra, we now encounter the second chakra, svadisthana. The roots of the muladhara and svadisthana chakras are located close together so that some functions are shared. This chakra is related to the sacral nerve plexus.

GOD: VISNU   GODDESS: SAKTI RAKINI

RIGHT A PICTORIAL
REPRESENTATION OF THE
CORRESPONDENCES FOR THE
SACRAL CHAKRA TAKEN FROM
KUNDALINI YOGA FOR THE WEST.

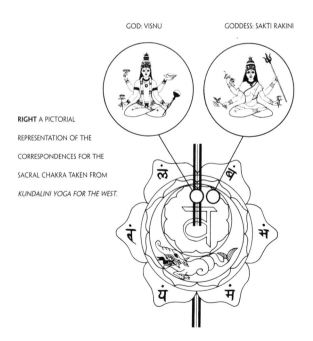

THE SACRAL CHAKRA: TABLE OF CORRESPONDENCES

LOCATION: The sacral plexus

SANSKRIT NAME: Svadisthana, meaning 'sweetness', or 'one's own abode'

ELEMENT: Water

FUNCTION: Pleasure, sexuality, procreation, creativity

INNER STATE: Self-confidence, well-being

BODY PARTS: Womb, kidneys, reproductive system, circulation system, bladder

GLANDS: Ovaries, Testicles

MALFUNCTION: Impotence, frigidity, uterine, bladder or kidney trouble

COLOUR: Orange

SEED SOUND: Vam

SENSE: Taste

PETALS: Six: bam, bham, mam, yam, ram, lam

ANIMAL SYMBOLS: Makara, fish, sea creatures

DEITIES: Vishnu, Rakini

ABOVE THE FISH SYMBOLIZES THE WATERY CHARACTERISTICS OF THE SACRAL CHAKRA.

FUNCTIONS OF THE SACRAL CHAKRA

This chakra is located within the abdomen, midway between the pubis and the navel. It governs sexuality, procreation and creativity at all levels. Inactive until puberty, this chakra affects the flow of fluids in the body: the circulation of blood, the production of urine, menstrual flow and the production of seminal fluids. Blockages or imbalances can cause disruption in any of these systems. This chakra is also connected with the kidney, bladder and triple heater meridians. The svadisthana chakra also has a profound bearing on certain states of mind. If the chakra is overly yang there can be undue emphasis on sexual activity joined to excessive fantasy. If the chakra is overly yin, impotence or other sexual problems can appear. Frustration, both sexual and creative, can be generated here when the life energies are blocked.

Sexuality and spirituality are usually considered to be worlds apart. Those who enter the spiritual life as monks, priests or nuns give up a sex life and become celibate choosing instead to channel the emotions through a life of service. Celibacy is inextricably bound to the religious values of the tradition itself. In the past some faiths, notably Christianity, promulgated celibacy as a means of overcoming the so-called temptations of the flesh. This attitude has left its legacy. Sex can still be thought of as a defilement of spiritual purity. The sex drive becomes the enemy within; it must be defeated at all cost. The practices that developed to keep the second chakra under control remain punitive, dour and repressive.

By contrast, it is possible to follow the path of celibacy by transmuting the sex drive rather than seeking to destroy it. This is a more positive and accepting approach. The life energies that are generated through the second chakra circulate upwards into the higher chakras, like a rising head of steam. Sexuality is transmuted; the energies that would have been available for a personal relationship are now freed and become available on a far wider basis. Life energies can flow to the many, not merely to the one.

The sexual energies can be aligned to the higher centres, especially to the fifth centre. The Tibetan states that when the energies of the sacral centre 'are reorientated and carried up to the throat centre, then the aspirant becomes a conscious creative force in the higher worlds. He (she) enters within the veil and begins to create the pattern of things which will bring about eventually the new heavens and the new earth'.

When this chakra awakens it brings increased powers of intuition and increasing psychic abilities. It is also said to bring awareness of the astral form. Awakening this chakra can affect the sex drive dramatically, either positively or negatively. In each case the effects are usually short-lived and stabilize as the energies settle. When this chakra is balanced it brings a sense of self-confidence and creativity. The imagination is used constructively and sexual energy brings a sense of completeness and integration.

ORIENTATION EXERCISES

1 How do you use the function of sexuality? What meaning does it have for you?
2 Meditate on the element of water.

ASANAS

THE LOCUST POSE (SHALHALABASANA)

1 Lie on your stomach with your hands beside your thighs with palms down.
2 Stretch and raise your legs with your abdomen as high as possible keeping the knees straight. Hold for a few seconds and then lower to the floor.

Repeat up to five times.

BELOW THE LOCUST POSE WORKS ON THE ABDOMEN TO STIMULATE THE SACRAL CHAKRA.

THE CAT-COW POSE

1   Place your hands and knees on the floor, so that you are making
    a bridge with your back.
2   Inhale, arch the back and raise your head.
3   Exhale, round the back and drop the head downwards. Establish
    a rhythm of inhaling, head up and exhaling, head down.
    Continue this for about one minute.

This exercise works on points along the spine including governor
vessels 3,4 and 5. These points are called the Gates of Life.

LEFT STRETCHING THE SPINE IN THE
CAT-COW ASANA WORKS ON THE
ACUPUNCTURE POINTS ALONG IT.

67

LEG-LIFTS

1   Lie on your back and relax.
2   Lift your legs about six inches away from the floor.
3   Spread them apart a little, bring the legs together and
    then kick out.

VISUALIZATION:
THE WOMB OF THE MOTHER

Darkness surrounds you, yet the dark feels comforting and safe. You
are floating suspended in water. You are immersed in water,
surrounded and held by water. You feel safe here, floating in these
warm waters. You are in the womb, deep in the womb of the one who
nurtured you. You are surrounded by her body, held in her waters.

You move and sway floating in your bubble. Here there are no thoughts, no fears, just life, growing, changing, developing. Life grows within the waters, quietly unfolding according to the pattern. You are surrounded by another's life, beyond the waters. This great being surrounds you with her love. You cannot name this feeling, nor understand it. But you grow in its presence as time passes. You feel safe, surrounded by love, immersed in love, floating in the waters. Time has no meaning for you but time passes and the waters change.

You know the waters in a deep primal sense, as you know no other element. You grew and were nourished by the waters. You floated in the waters while nine moons passed. You filled the waters and were finally born from them. You have no conscious memory of that time spent in the darkness of the waters, yet your consciousness can remember the feelings of that blissful state. Every human being has passed this way too. Every human being begins in the darkness and the waters. There is no other way into life.

TIPS FOR WORKING WITH THE SACRAL CHAKRA

DREAM IMAGES

This chakra tends to produce dreams in which water images appear: images of pools, lakes, streams, rivers and seas. The quality of the water is indicative of the way in which this chakra is functioning. Stagnant, dirty or foul water requires inner cleansing. Frozen water, ice in any form requires thawing. Images of bathing or washing are indicative that a cleansing process has commenced. Swimming indicates ease with the functions of this chakra. Drowning indicates difficulties. Fountains or gushing waters indicate the sudden or unexpected awaking of this chakra. Meetings with creatures or beings who are at home in the waters and are willing to act as guides indicate that the individual is integrating some aspect of this chakra.

Dreams in which the moon plays a prominent part are also related to this chakra: travelling to the moon or exploring a lunar landscape indicates inner exploration at this level.

BACH FLOWER REMEDIES

Crab apple	10	Getting rid of what you cannot digest
Elm	11	Turning your ideas into reality
Mimulus	20	Freedom within a structure
Oak	22	Surrender
Vervain	31	Accepting others
Wild rose	37	Taking part joyfully in life

RIGHT THE MIMULUS BACH FLOWER REMEDY CAN HELP YOU TO ACHIEVE A SENSE OF FREEDOM IN YOUR LIFE.

69

MUSIC

Sensual flowing music is appropriate here. Listen to traditional music for belly dancing. This has the power to release the energies of this chakra.

THE GATEWAY
OF THE SUN

CHAPTER SIX

The abdomen contains the digestive system, which transmutes food into energy. We rarely think about this process, except when it malfunctions in some way. Food provides fuel for the body. Just as the physical digestive system extracts energy from food, so the solar plexus chakra extracts and stores prana. Prana is the energy that permeates all life; where there is prana there is life. Each of the chakras is a centre of prana, but it is generated and distributed by the manipura centre. Prana can be directed to any of the body's systems through the power of the directed imagination in conjunction with a sound knowledge of anatomy.

LEFT THE SYMBOL FOR PRANA, THE ENERGY THAT PERMEATES ALL LIFE, WHICH IS STORED IN THE SOLAR PLEXUS CHAKRA.

FUNCTIONS OF THE
SOLAR PLEXUS CHAKRA

Physically this chakra governs the stomach and digestive system. The manipura chakra relates to the liver, gall bladder, stomach and spleen. Imbalances can give rise to eating or

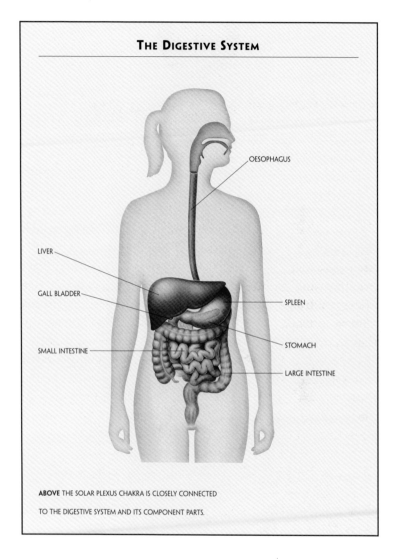

THE DIGESTIVE SYSTEM

OESOPHAGUS

LIVER

GALL BLADDER

SPLEEN

SMALL INTESTINE

STOMACH

LARGE INTESTINE

ABOVE THE SOLAR PLEXUS CHAKRA IS CLOSELY CONNECTED
TO THE DIGESTIVE SYSTEM AND ITS COMPONENT PARTS.

digestive disorders. Ulcers, which are frequently related to high
levels of stress, are a classic disorder of this centre.

The solar plexus chakra is our place of empowerment in the world.
It is the personal fuel store. If the fuel store is low, we lack the driving
force to project ourselves into the world with impact. We become

THE SOLAR PLEXUS CHAKRA:
TABLE OF CORRESPONDENCES

LOCATION: Rooted between the twelfth thoracic vertebra and first lumbar vertebra

SANSKRIT NAME: Manipura, meaning 'lustrous gem' or 'city of jewels'

ELEMENT: Fire

FUNCTION: Will, power

INNER STATE: Intense emotion: laughter, joy, anger

BODY PARTS: Digestive system, liver, spleen, stomach, small intestine

GLANDS: Pancreas

MALFUNCTION: Ulcers, diabetes, eating disorders such as anorexia and bulimia, hypoglycaemia

COLOUR: Yellow

SEED SOUND: Ram

SENSE: Sight

PETALS: Ten: da, dha, na, ta, tha, da, dha, na, pa, pha

ANIMAL SYMBOLS: Ram

DEITIES: Rudra, Lakini, Apollo, Agni

victims of fate and circumstance when we lose touch with will power, which is a direct expression of inner being. The will is fundamental to well-being and personal fulfilment, translating our innermost nature into outer expression, enabling us to overcome difficult life circumstances. If an individual is weak-willed, the qualities of self-determination and self-direction are undeveloped. They are easily swayed from any given course by the influence of others. If someone is wilful, they exercise power with total disregard to others. It is through the expression of will that we create our own reality: our power in the world is an expression of our sense of will.

GOD: VISNU   GODDESS: LAKINI

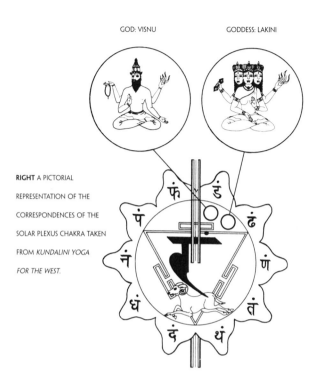

RIGHT A PICTORIAL
REPRESENTATION OF THE
CORRESPONDENCES OF THE
SOLAR PLEXUS CHAKRA TAKEN
FROM *KUNDALINI YOGA*
FOR THE WEST.

When the will is blocked we experience a sense of frustration, which is often accompanied by a tightening of the whole solar plexus area. When we lose our sense of power, the stomach seems to turn to water. Our strength vanishes, our fire has been extinguished. Ideally there should be a free flow of energy between the personal will and the freedom to project in the world, but this is often blocked. It can be a temporary obstacle created by a personal dispute or it can be a longer-lasting situation of repression. Accord between inner comprehension of personal will and outer freedom of expression allows the energy of the third chakra to flow evenly. When the will is blocked, either at source or externally, the chakra cannot release and energies begin to impact. The chakra acts like a dam holding back feelings, energies, needs and drives. There is inner turmoil, repressed anger and contained force. Eventually something snaps and there is an emotional scene, a crisis, even a breakdown. Traditionally the awakening of this chakra is said to bring the power to locate hidden treasure. This is an interesting correspondence with the actual name of this chakra, lustrous gem. It may also have a symbolic meaning indicating that spiritual reality itself is the hidden treasure. The awakening of this chakra is said to confer mastery over fire. This refers to the internal fires and to the generation of psychic heat through controlled use of natural energy. The ability to see the body from within is also said to develop as the functions of this chakra unfold.

ORIENTATION EXERCISES

1 Explore the concept of personal power by considering
   how you use power in the world.
2 Meditate on the element of fire.

When the energies of this chakra are active and balanced, the individual enjoys well-being and has a clear sense of personal self-determination.

PRANAYAMA EXERCISES

JOINING THE STREAMS

1 Sit with a straight spine.
2 Inhale deeply. Imagine prana being absorbed through your
   throat and flowing down to your navel.
3 At the same time imagine apana flowing up from the muladhara
   to the navel. Assume mula banda (perineum lock) and visualize
   the two streams uniting at the navel.

You might also work on 'The Breath of Fire' and 'Hara Breathing'.

Asanas

BELLY PUSH

1 Sit with your legs outstretched, hands flat on the floor underneath your shoulders.
2 Lift your body by raising your buttocks.
3 Make a straight line with your body from the toes to the head.
    4 Drop back to a seated position and repeat.

LEFT LIFT YOUR BODY BY RAISING YOUR BUTTOCKS TO MAKE A STRAIGHT LINE FROM TOES TO HEAD.

SPINAL FLEXES

This exercise flexes the spine in both directions.

1 Sit on your heels with your hands on your knees and curve your back.
2 Inhale and arch your back. Push your chest up and out.
3 Exhale as you slump down. Repeat the cycle.

RIGHT AND LEFT REGULAR PRACTICE OF SPINAL FLEXES HELPS TO INCREASE THE FLEXIBILITY AND MOBILITY OF THE SPINE.

THE PINCERS (PASCHIMOTTANASANA)

1   Sit on the floor with your legs extended, arms on thighs.

2   Slowly bend your upper torso forwards, sliding your hands along the legs. Bend forward as far as is comfortable; ideally the forehead should touch the knees.

ABOVE IN THIS ASANA, THE HEAD SHOULD BE AS CLOSE TO THE KNEES AS POSSIBLE WITHOUT STRAINING.

VISUALIZATION: GREETING THE SUN

Find yourself standing on a high outcrop of rock in a barren treeless landscape. It is still quite dark; dawn is about to break. Your vantage point enables you to look out across the land. Even in this light you are able to see a vast desert plain stretching in every direction. Here and there you see huge stony outcrops like fingers reaching up into the sky. At the distant edge of the horizon, the sun begins to rise. You watch as the great ball of fire shows itself. It seems red in colour as it comes into view. You raise your arms in greeting

RIGHT A VISUALIZATION OF THE SUN'S LIGHT AND WARMTH

CAN HELP TO ACTIVATE THE SOLAR PLEXUS CHAKRA.

TIPS FOR WORKING WITH THE SOLAR PLEXUS CHAKRA

DREAM IMAGES

This chakra produces a wide array of fiery images: setting a fire; preparing a ritual fire, watching a house on fire; even being on fire but paradoxically being unharmed. Images of sunrise or other solar images can be indicative of an awakening at this level.

BACH FLOWER REMEDIES

Aspen	2	Overcoming fears
Hornbeam	17	Being able to achieve personal goals
Impatiens	18	Patience
Larch	19	Self-awareness
Scleranthus	28	Balance within yourself
Star of Bethlehem	29	Ability to act from joy

77

LEFT THE IMPATIENS BACH FLOWER REMEDY HELPS TO GIVE PATIENCE TO A PERSON WHOSE SOLAR PLEXUS CHAKRA IS BLOCKED.

MUSIC

This chakra is concerned with expressing emotions. When emotions are not released at the appropriate time the vibration quite literally becomes lodged in the chakra and the body. Music that has the power to express an emotion, whether it is grief or joy, can provide a much needed cathartic experience. You might like to listen to *Sunrise* by David Sun, *The Enchanter* by Tim Wheater and *Aquamarine* by Stairway.

as this great being emerges from the darkness of night. Sunlight begins to flood the terrain, lighting up the seemingly endless vista. You feel a touch of warmth on your face as the sun's rays lengthen.

As the sun rises higher into the sky, changing in colour from red to a burning yellow, it seems to ignite the spark within your own fire centre. Your mind becomes filled with the image of a radiating sphere deep within your centre of being. It glows with brightness that spreads outward as you stand upon your high peak. It rises within you as a great fiery ball emerging from slumber. You begin to breathe deeply, drinking in the rays of the sun like a liquid gold. As you breathe in you are filled with a shower of brilliance. As you breathe out, you radiate this divine energy towards other living forms. As you stand in the ever-increasing brightness of a new day, become aware of the living quality of the whole landscape. In the freshness of the new dawn everything radiates life. As you continue with your deep breathing your inhalations seem to put you in touch with the very life force of the land, the stones, the sand and the air itself. As you breathe in you feel that you are drinking in the power that the land has to offer you, sharing in its daily cycle of renewal. This force fills your power centre, flooding you with vital life force. You feel wholly alive, empowered, exhilarated. Your own energy store is now full to overflowing. Take this power into your life and use it to be fulfilled.

THE GATEWAY
OF THE WINDS

CHAPTER SEVEN

Rising up from the solar plexus we now encounter the heart chakra. Its name anahata means unstruck or unbeaten. It refers to a sound that is heard yet is not struck, in other words an eternal note which is not made by human hands. This allusion to the eternal marks the entry, which takes place at this centre, into higher levels of consciousness.

FUNCTIONS OF THE HEART CHAKRA

The symbolism of the heart as the place of love is also obvious. The associations between the heart and the experience of love are deeply engrained in our culture. It is almost impossible to think of one without the other. We send cards decorated with hearts on Valentine's Day and we are heartbroken if we lose our love. A lonely heart speaks for itself. The Sacred Heart, now a name for many convents and schools, symbolizes transcendent Christian love. We are each more familiar with the love of interpersonal relationships than with universal love.

LEFT THE HEART AND THE EMOTION OF LOVE ARE DEEPLY CONNECTED IN OUR CULTURE.

THE HEART CHAKRA: TABLE OF CORRESPONDENCES

LOCATION: Rooted between the fourth and fifth thoracic vertebrae

SANSKRIT NAME: Anahata, meaning 'unstruck'

ELEMENT: Air

FUNCTION: Love

INNER STATE: Compassion, love

BODY PARTS: Lungs, heart, arms, hands

GLANDS: Thymus

MALFUNCTION: Asthma, blood pressure, heart disease, lung disease

COLOUR: Green

SEED SOUND: Lam

SENSE: Touch

PETALS: Twelve: kam, kham, gam, gham, ngam, cham, chham, jam, jham, nyam, tam, than

ANIMAL SYMBOLS: Antelope, birds, dove

ABOVE BIRDS ARE ONE OF THE ANIMAL SYMBOLS FOR THE HEART CHAKRA.

At first sight this seems to be the easiest chakra to understand. Yet it often turns out to be the place where we are the least active in reality. We have each experienced falling in and out of love, we each love and are surely loved in return. Yet personal love is just the starting point for the experience of this chakra. The quality, degree and form of love assigned to the fourth chakra is quite different from personal love. For the most part we aim to bring love into our lives, instinctively acknowledging the goodness within the experience of loving. We instinctively recognize both its presence and its absence. Everyone needs to be loved and to give love in return. Without love there is true deprivation and a warping of natural development.

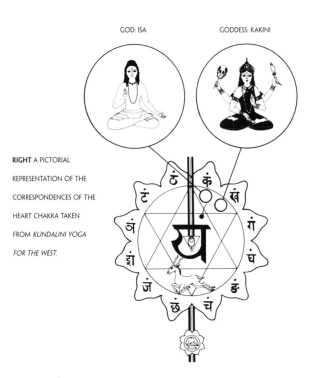

GOD: ISA GODDESS: KAKINI

RIGHT A PICTORIAL REPRESENTATION OF THE CORRESPONDENCES OF THE HEART CHAKRA TAKEN FROM *KUNDALINI YOGA FOR THE WEST.*

The heart centre is not easy to fully awaken. Our love is so easily limited to family, friends, to those who love us in return. Many grow up in loveless and unloving homes and have no experience of being nurtured and valued. Even personalized love at its most giving and open-hearted is but a reflection of a universal and unlimited love.

The heart centre is unique in having a subsidiary chakra, which is represented within a lotus of eight petals beneath the anahata chakra. This subsidiary chakra is called the Kalpavriksha or Kalpa tree and is known as the celestial wish-fulfilling tree. It is said to function only when the anahata has been awakened first. This centre is said to grant personal wishes, but paradoxically if this centre has truly awakened, the heart's desire will be for the happiness and good of others. The anahata centre controls the sense of touch. This is not surprising, for the heart meridians run along the length of the arms into the hands.

It is through our hands that we offer love in the form of comfort, a loving caress or a healing touch. Prana is most easily radiated through the hands and with appropriate visualization it can be directed from the heart centre itself. The individual develops an increasingly subtle sense of touch, which enables the energy field of others to be directly sensed.

ABOVE OPENING UP THE HEART CENTRE INCREASES OUR SENSITIVITY TO TOUCH.

The previous centres are closely bound up with personal and group karma. Opening the lower three chakras inevitably releases karmic forces. However, the anahata chakra is not subordinate to karmic influences. The individual stands above and outside the bounds of karma. The path towards higher consciousness begins at this level, where karma no longer binds and universal life is experienced.

The activation of this centre brings many different qualities. As this centre opens it brings an increasingly subtle sense of touch. The individual becomes highly sensitized to the energy fields of others and it becomes possible to detect areas where there is disturbance and disease simply through the refinement of touch. The ability to heal is a natural extension of the increased capacity for love. Prana is easily directed through the hands in a healing contact. Psychokinesis can also develop when the anahata awakens. The power to love impersonally and without discrimination remains the central quality of this chakra, however. It is from this expansion of love that all other qualities naturally flow.

When this chakra is open and balanced there is a genuine ability to give and to receive. Compassion develops and becomes a natural expression of feeling.

ORIENTATION EXERCISES

1   Explore your own experiences of giving and receiving love.

2   Meditate on the element of air.

ASANAS

FLAPPING WINGS

1   Stand with your arms outstretched.

2   Stretch your arms backwards without bending the elbows so
    that you feel a pressure in your shoulder blades.

ABOVE THIS ASANA HELPS TO RELEASE BLOCKAGES IN THE HEART CHAKRA.

3 Keep bending your hands backward.

4 Inhale and raise your chest up and outwards. Exhale: keeping the arms outstretched bring your palms together in front of you, curving the spine slightly forward.

5 Take your hands back on the inhalation.

6 Bring them forward on the exhalation.

This wonderfully dynamic exercise is helpful for releasing constrictions in the chest area. It stimulates the points normally used to treat cardiovascular problems. It also counteracts rounded shoulders and slumped postures, which are so often produced by sedentary work.

CROSSING THE HEART

1 Sit cross-legged if possible.

2 Place your right hand in the left armpit and your left hand in the right armpit.

3 Close your eyes and feel your heart beating.

4 Attempt to locate the heart space and meditate upon it. The vision of the blue lake and blue lotus may appear during this pose.

RIGHT THE CROSSING THE
HEART MEDITATION
EXERCISE HELPS YOU TO FOCUS
ON THE HEART CHAKRA.

OPENING THE HEART

1 Stand straight, with the feet shoulder-width apart.

2 Breathe deeply and raise the arms above the head.

3 Bend backward, letting the head drop back. If you find this difficult, stand near a wall for support. Do not hold this pose for more than a few seconds at first. This is a surprisingly dynamic exercise which instantly reveals areas of restriction.

RIGHT THE BACKWARD STRETCH CAN WORK
DRAMATICALLY ON THE HEART CHAKRA.

VISUALIZATION:
THE ROSE OF THE HEART

Allow the mind to become quiet. Focus your awareness upon the area of the physical heart and its cavity. Although the physical heart occupies only a small space, the true heart is without limitations. Try to feel the beating of your own heart. Begin to think of the people that you are able to love. Allow their faces to rise up singly so that you are able to acknowledge each one individually. As you do this you may feel a sensation, even a tightness, around the heart. Look into the heart space and see the bud of a rose slowly unfolding. Watch the slow movement of the petals as the bloom grows within you. Continue to think about the people whom you love. Now think of those who love you. Watch the rose increasing in size. See the softness of the petals and beauty of its fresh

LEFT VISUALIZING UPON THE ROSE WILL HELP YOU TO
SEND OUT UNCONDITIONAL LOVE.

bloom. Allow the rose to complete its growing until it seems to fill your heart. Now radiate the love that you have accumulated. Let it stream out from the heart in a shaft of bright light. Let your love pour forth in a steady stream to those whose hearts are empty.

MEDITATION: FINDING THE HEART SPACE

Sit in a comfortable position for meditation. Close the eyes and concentrate on the throat. Breathe in with a deep full breath. Feel the breath filling the chest cavity. Allow the outgoing breath to pass without attention. Repeat this until you are fully focused on the breath. Next direct your attention to the space just above the diaphragm. Become aware of this space being filled. Gradually you will develop an awareness of this heart space. When you feel that you

TIPS FOR WORKING WITH THE HEART CHAKRA

DREAM IMAGES
The heart chakra can appear in dreams involving love: being in love, falling in love or even losing love. Such dreams often evoke a keenly-felt emotional response such as joy or deep sadness.

BACH FLOWER REMEDIES

Centuary	4	Service
Chicory	8	Overcoming distance
Heather	14	Unconditional love
Holly	15	Free-flowing love energy
Honeysuckle	16	Living in the here and now
Red chestnut	25	The ability to express true love
Rock rose	26	Overcoming ego limitations

MUSIC

This centre is concerned with making contact with the universalized power of love. Everyone is familiar with certain pieces of music which have the power to melt the heart. The natural sounds of whales and dolphins can take us beyond ourselves. Pachelbel's *Canon,* which is often used for circle dancing, is a wonderfully soothing and healing piece of music. You might also like to listen to these pieces with the heart, not the mind: *Great Piece* by Robert Martin, *Quiet Water* by Fitzgerald and Flanagan and *The Response* by John Richardson.

RIGHT DEEPLY MOVING MUSIC OR SOUNDS, SUCH AS THE COMMUNICATION OF DOLPHINS, CAN HELP TO OPEN THE HEART CHAKRA.

have discovered it, the heart space will expand and contract in time with the breath. If consciousness is maintained, the student will spontaneously see a vision of a blue lake and a blue lotus. This vision will appear at the right time. Do not use the power of the creative imagination to build the scene.

THE GATEWAY OF TIME AND SPACE

CHAPTER EIGHT

The throat chakra represents our power to communicate verbally. The development of speech is unique to humanity, even though many other species have developed subtle and sophisticated ways of communication. Speech and the wide range of human vocalization permits communication of a complex and unique kind. The human voice can convey emotion, information and a huge range of subtle meanings. We can sing, shout, whisper or laugh; we can cry or scream. The human voice can conceal the truth or reveal the truth. It is often possible to detect a lie in the voice; there is a lack of certainty and a quality of falsity.

FUNCTIONS OF THE THROAT CHAKRA

The function of hearing is assigned to this chakra, and refers to a subtle quality of inner hearing that is quite different from our ordinary day-to-day physical hearing. By tradition the opening of this chakra brings increased telepathic rapport. Telepathy can be thought of as hearing inwardly, which is something that we all do from time to time. Usually this is no more than a fleeting, often unconscious experience. The activation of this chakra, however, brings telepathy into consciousness.

THE THROAT CHAKRA: TABLE OF CORRESPONDENCES

LOCATION: The throat

SANSKRIT NAME: Vishuddha, meaning 'to purify'

ELEMENT: Akasa

FUNCTION: Creativity, communication

INNER STATE: Intuition, synthesis

BODY PARTS: Neck, shoulders

GLANDS: Thyroid and parathyroid

MALFUNCTION: Sore throat, swollen glands, colds, thyroid problems

COLOUR: Bright blue

SEED SOUND: Ham

SENSE: Hearing

PETALS: Sixteen: A, Ā, I, Ī, U, Ū, Ṛ, Ṛ, L, Ḷ, E, ai, 0, au, am, ah

ANIMALS: Elephant

DEITIES: Sadasiva; Sakini, an aspect of Gauri

The poet, writer and storyteller all instinctively understand the power of the word, whether spoken or written, and employ this power to evoke a personal response. Those working in mass media also understand the persuasive powers of communication and use the vehicle of the word to shape group consciousness. We are surrounded, indeed submerged, by words. We live in an age of mass communication and mass communicators. Paradoxically, this sea of sound has the effect of deadening our senses, dulling rather than sharpening our powers of discrimination, blunting rather than

LEFT OUR ABILITY TO COMMUNICATE IS DIRECTLY AFFECTED BY THE THROAT CHAKRA.

sharpening our critical faculties. Spiritual traditions have on the other hand kept alive the value of the word by preserving a place for silence through non-verbal contemplative practices. It remains only too easy to speak without thinking, to waste words and to utter empty phrases. Discovering the power of effective genuine communication is one of the tasks presented by this chakra.

The vishuddha chakra functions in conjunction with two other minor centres, the lalana at the base of the nasal orifice and the bindu vishargha at the top of the brain towards the back of the head. Hindu monks are usually shaven except for a small tuft of hair which marks this spot. Its name means 'the falling of drops'. The sahasrara chakra secretes drops described as nectar which collect within the bindu. These then pass on to the lalana at the base of the

GOD: SADASIVA   GODDESS: GAURI (ETERNAL)

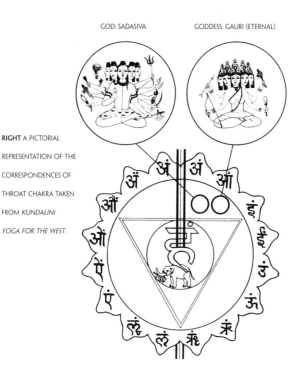

RIGHT A PICTORIAL REPRESENTATION OF THE CORRESPONDENCES OF THROAT CHAKRA TAKEN FROM *KUNDALINI YOGA FOR THE WEST.*

nasal orifice. If the vishuddha has been awakened the drops undergo purification and then have the power to rejuvenate the body. As the divine nectar is purified, extraordinary metabolic control becomes a possibility. Yogis have in the past been buried for as long as 40 days to test themselves in a state of suspended animation. In preparation for this trial, the tendon beneath the tongue is gradually severed so that the tongue is curled back in the epiglottis to seal the respiratory passage. This directly stimulates the lalana to secrete more nectar which falls to the vishuddha where it is distributed throughout the body.

There is a link between the development of inner hearing and the process of creativity. Creative artists often perceive themselves as receivers tuned in to a particular wavelength that is not of their making. Some writers experience a kind of inner dictation; others have inspirational dreams. Musicians invariably hear music inwardly. The creative process can be like a powerful over-shadowing or possession, so often the creative artist admits to feeling like an instrument of a greater power that in every respect appears to be external.

Esoteric teachings tell us that when the throat chakra is inactive, our creativity will likewise be subdued. We will be unable to hear inwardly, or outwardly to give form to originality. In other words, we are inoperative as creative channels.

When this chakra is open and balanced, the powers of communication and creativity come to life, adding a new dimension to our comprehension of experience.

ORIENTATION EXERCISES

1 Explore your own powers of communication by reflecting on what you say and how you say it.
2 Meditate on the element of akasa.

ASANAS

SIDE TO SIDE

1 Lie comfortably on your back; inhale deeply.

2 Exhale and slowly turn your head to the left.

3 Inhale as your head returns to the centre.

4 Exhale as you turn your head to the right.

5 Continue this exercise for one minute, gently stretching your neck from side to side.

This simple exercise opens up the neck and stimulates the thyroid gland.

BRIDGE

1 Lie comfortably on your back with your legs bent and the bottoms of your feet flat on the floor; keep your hands by your sides.

2 Inhale, bringing your hands off the floor to support the hips and pelvis.

3 Lift your pelvis upwards.

4 Exhale and lower your body down to the starting position.

5 Exercise for one minute.

ABOVE AS THE PELVIS IS LIFTED DURING THE BRIDGE ASANA, THE THROAT AND THYROID ARE STIMULATED.

SHOULDER STAND

1   Lie down on your back; inhale
    and bend your knees towards
    your chest.
2   Exhale and swing your legs
    upwards so that your hips lift up
    from the floor.
3   Use your hands to support your
    lower back.
4   Straighten your legs and your
    back as much as possible.
5   Begin long, deep breathing.

This asana causes subtle changes in
the prana flow in the body and it
facilitates the flow from manipura to
vishuddha. This is also an important
posture for transferring sexual
energies from the lower to the higher
dimensions. This asana should not be
performed during menstruation. It
should be performed with a firm
support, either a foam Yoga block or a
folded blanket placed beneath the shoulders, so that the neck and
throat are slightly lower than the shoulders before the posture starts.
This prevents the throat becoming constricted during the posture.

ABOVE MAKE SURE THAT THE SHOULDERS ARE
SUPPORTED DURING THE SHOULDER STAND SO
THAT THE THROAT IS NOT CONSTRICTED.

93

AWAKENING THE BINDU VISHARGA

1   Sit in a meditational pose with the eyes closed.
2   Be aware of the natural breathing for some two minutes.
3   Use the mantra 'so ham'. Repeat 'so' on the inbreath and 'ham'
    on the outbreath. Place the sound in the throat.
4   Maintain awareness of the breath and the mantra together in a
    continuous rhythm.

5   Place the mantra in a straight line between the throat and a point at the top of the head towards the back.

6   On the inhalation imagine a thread of white light extending from the vishuddha to the bindu.

As these centres awaken, psychic sound, which is inaudible to physical hearing, can be heard around the bindu. This will indicate its location more precisely.

RIGHT BY REGULARLY PRACTISING THE BINDU VISHARGA MEDITATION, YOU WILL AWAKEN YOUR ABILITY TO HEAR PSYCHIC SOUND.

94

VISUALIZATION: THE WOMB OF SPACE

Allow your surroundings to dissolve. Imagine that you stand before a great white wall. Step closer and place your hands upon it. You will find that it is not dense and solid but light as if made from a gossamer fabric stretched taut. Place your hands gently against the soft surface and feel it billowing against your hands. Take hold of the substance with both hands. Allow the wish to pass through the veil to rise within you.

As the thought is created so the veil opens between your hands creating a doorway shaped like a vesica piscis. You look beyond the veil and see the darkness and the wonder of deep space lit by points of white light. You make a choice to step back and close the veil or to step out into the unknown.

If you decide to return, simply step back and close the veil. If you wish to carry on, step out with trust. You float in the silence of space. You are supported by space itself. The sensation is disconcerting, but if you surrender to your weightlessness you can begin to enjoy the new experience. You float effortlessly observing what you can in this strange silent world. Bright stars pepper the sky in every direction; some seem so close that you feel you might be able to touch them.

As you float you suddenly and unexpectedly become aware of a sound. It startles you momentarily. It is a note that seems to come from everywhere at once. Now you lie back and listen, trying to hear the sound more clearly. The note seems to swell in volume and to become more complex in some way. You are surrounded by the sound, which continues to reverberate. Now a new sound emerges. It is the sound of your name. You hear your name in a new way yet you cannot fail to recognize the vibration that is your name. You may answer if you wish, not with your voice but with your mind. The sound repeats over and over again like a mantra deep in space.

You seem able to sense the vibrations that your name creates. Your body begins to sway gently, rocked by unseen patterns of sound. You no longer float without direction. The power of sound carries you along on a wave which rises and falls with the patterns of your name. Your body sways on this sea of sound, gently propelled along by the vibrating notes themselves. Your body itself begins to vibrate. Your whole being takes up the resonance in harmony with the sounds that support you. As the resonance deepens you feel as if the very sound sloughs away the outworn and superfluous aspects of your existence that cling to you like a second skin. The sound continues its cleansing process, raising your vibrations to the pure sound of your true name. Now you seem to be moving along with ease propelled by waves of sound.

Ahead of you see the white gossamer veil with the open portal. Your journey nears its end. You have a last opportunity to express

TIPS FOR WORKING WITH THE THROAT CHAKRA

DREAM IMAGES

The images that relate to this chakra often involve visits to foreign or strange places: mountain tops, hidden lands, or quiet alien landscapes. In such dreams, contact is often made with a foreign race that appears to be superior in wisdom and understanding. Teaching is often offered either formally or informally. In the dream the content of this teaching carries great weight, yet paradoxically it seems difficult to recall it upon waking.

BACH FLOWER REMEDIES

Agrimony	1	Fusing thinking and feeling
Mustard	21	Trusting your self even in the face of adversity
Wild oat	3	Communicating from your deepest levels
Willow	38	Making space for creativity

LEFT THE AGRIMONY BACH FLOWER REMEDY CAN HELP TO ACHIEVE A BALANCE BETWEEN THE THOUGHT AND FEELING PROCESSES.

MUSIC

This centre expresses both the creativity of the individual and the spaciousness of the group. Immerse yourself in the sound of massed voices whether choirs or sacred chant. Lose yourself in the whole and paradoxically find your own note.

something, to speak with your inner voice. You reach the portal, carried gently all the way. You simply step through the opening and touch terra firma again. It feels good to return but it also feels good to have journeyed.

THE GATEWAY OF LIBERATION

CHAPTER NINE

W e now rise up to the centre commonly associated with the third eye, the ajna chakra. The ajna chakra is located at the junction of the ida, pingala and sushumna meridians, at the brow. The confluence of the three energies brings extraordinary gifts once awakened. Sushumna alone rises upwards into the crown. Ida and pingala terminate at this junction. This is the underlying truth behind the idea of the third eye with which so many people are familiar. This centre certainly acts as a third eye when awakened. Its name 'to know' refers to aspects of telepathy and other means of direct knowing which bypass the ordinary senses. At this level immediate perception is a possibility. The barriers that circumscribe the self have long since been transcended. Just as a sighted person in a crowd of blind people would naturally have the advantage that sight brings, the awakened ajna chakra is the eye of the soul bringing all-round vision.

FUNCTIONS OF THE BROW CHAKRA

The ajna chakra brings freedom at many levels. Its liberation lies in the fact that it represents a state of consciousness in which there are no divisions and no limitations. It is outside and beyond

THE BROW CHAKRA: TABLE OF CORRESPONDENCES

LOCATION: The brow, just above the bridge of the nose

SANSKRIT NAME: Ajna, meaning 'to know', 'to perceive' or 'to command'.

ELEMENT: None applicable

FUNCTION: Direct perception

INNER STATE: Self-mastery

BODY PARTS: Eyes, two hemispheres of the brain

GLAND: Pituitary

MALFUNCTION: Headaches, nightmares, defects of vision

COLOUR: Indigo

SEED SOUND: Om

SENSE: None applicable

PETALS: Two

ANIMALS: None applicable

DEITIES: Paramasiva (Shiva in the highest form) and Sakti Hakini

all constraints. The state of consciousness represented by the ajna chakra is also beyond all personal karmic influences. The individual who has awakened the forces of the ajna chakra is able to use the energies to help the karmic situation of others. This is a most extraordinary concept which raises all sorts of questions. Motoyama himself tells us that after his awakening he became aware of the karma not only of individuals, but also of larger entities such as families and nations. He discovered that he had the power to beneficially affect the karma of others. Motoyama considered this to be the most important aspect of the awakening of this chakra. Christ himself said that he could wash away the sins of the world, in other words that he could dissolve the accumulated karma of humanity.

GOD/GODDESS: SAKTI HAKINI

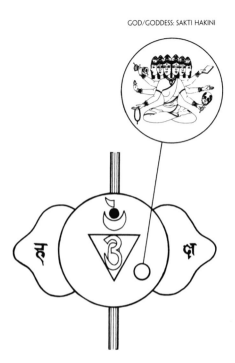

100

ABOVE A PICTORIAL REPRESENTATION OF THE CORRESPONDENCES OF
THE BROW CHAKRA TAKEN FROM *KUNDALINI YOGA FOR THE WEST.*

Satyananda suggests that this chakra needs to be awakened first so
that spiritual contact of a high level is established prior to releasing
the karmic energies related to the other chakras. By becoming
conscious at this level, it is possible to stand above karma and gain
a complete understanding of it through wisdom and not the
process of catharsis.

The activation of this chakra increases the powers of visualization,
which can be thought of as the power to see with the mind's eye. We
each have a natural facility for creating images; the mind
spontaneously produces images as part of the dreaming process.
Children often have a vivid imagination that inevitably dulls with
maturation and education. We were each once children with vivid

imaginations, but we have invariably lost the quality to react to the world in a whole way, substituting instead the representational code of words rather than pictures. The value of visualization seems to lie in its ability to involve the whole person in any given response. The picture-making facility has the power to evoke not merely the image itself but also a constellation of emotions and feelings. The image-producing abilities are centred in the right hemisphere of the brain, which is also responsible for emotional responses and symbolic representations of the world. It seems to be this fact that makes visualization such a powerful tool in so many respects. Visualization is a key component in certain forms of meditation. It is a significant factor in self-healing and in psychic unfoldment.

The chakras of the mind, the ajna and the sahasrara, naturally relate to the two endocrine glands within the head, the pituitary and the pineal. There is, however, a long-standing debate over the attribution. Some authorities attribute the ajna chakra to the pineal gland, others attribute it to the pituitary gland. The pineal gland is a tiny cone-shaped structure. Its real function remains a mystery. In birds the pineal gland seems to be connected with the ability to navigate using the amount of available light as a reference. Alice Bailey sets out a good case for the ajna being attributed to the pituitary gland, which is the command centre for the endocrine system as a whole. The pituitary gland is called the 'master gland' by certain yogic texts because it is said to have the power to rejuvenate the entire system. The pituitary works in conjunction with the hypothalamus to release 12 separate hormones that affect a wide range of vital functions including the repair of body tissue, patterns of sleep, breast feeding, uterine contractions during labour, and sexual maturation. In terms of physiological development the pituitary is vital. Furthermore the pituitary is divided into two distinct parts reminiscent of the two petals allocated to this chakra, the anterior and posterior lobes. My own preference after much thought is to attribute the ajna chakra to the pituitary gland and the crown chakra to the pineal gland.

THE POWER OF VISUALIZATION

You can easily try out the power of visualization for yourself in a small way. Start by naming something out loud for yourself. It could be anything simple such as a rose, a car or a tree. When you have named your chosen item, study your own response. What response did this word evoke from you? Now close your eyes and see a picture of the same item with the mind's eye. Create the image as clearly as you can and evaluate the image in the same way. What response did the image evoke from you? Now compare the effect of the spoken word with that of the created image. You will surely notice a qualitative difference in your own response. When visualization is allied to real-life issues it has the power to evoke a deep-seated response which represents the total will of the individual. When visualization is allied to everyday thinking it seems to open the door to new levels of perception and awareness. If you visualize an image of your friend before phoning, the way the image forms in your mind might prove to be informative. If you have a genuine need for something in your life, spend time creating the relevant image in your mind on a regular basis. When your mind is familiar with thinking visually, it seems to create an internal blank screen, ever ready for the spontaneous projection of images. When images arise in this way one part of the mind seems to produce a picture which it then hands over to another part of the mind for interpretation.

ASANAS

The ajna chakra is activated indirectly by working with the forces of the muladhara centred at the perineum. The ajna and muladhara are

ORIENTATION EXERCISES

Try out your ability to visualize. The following exercise is very simple.

Sit comfortably, close your eyes and relax. Become aware of the fact that the brain is composed of two hemispheres. Visualize the number '1' in the left hemisphere and the letter 'A' in the right hemisphere. Next visualize '2' in the left hemisphere and 'B' in the right hemisphere. Continue until you reach '26' and 'Z'. Pause and enter deep relaxation. Breathe in and out through the ajna.

Now repeat the exercise by placing the letters in the left hemisphere and the numbers in the right. When you have done this you might like to compare the difference.

Now imagine the sun rising in the right hemisphere and setting in the left. Then imagine the moon rising in the left hemisphere and setting in the right. Relax and allow images that symbolize each of the hemispheres for you to spontaneously arise.

LEFT TRY VISUALIZING THE LEFT AND RIGHT SIDE OF THE BRAIN AND SEE WHAT IMAGES SPONTANEOUSLY OCCUR.

polar points upon the same axis. Ida, pingala and sushumna begin at muladhara and converge again at the ajna. The chakras are also linked by the same image, that of the inverted triangle which symbolizes the storehouse of creative energy.

AWAKENING THE EYE

1 Sit with your legs crossed so that one heel presses into the area of the perineum.

2 Place your hands on your knees, keeping the spine straight.

3   Concentrate at a point between your eyebrows. Begin alternately
     to contract and relax your perineum upon inhalation and
     exhalation.

4   Next, imagine prana being absorbed into the ajna centre on the
     inhalation. On the exhalation imagine prana as a stream of light
     being radiated outwards into the universe. Chant the mantra
     Om, the seed mantra for this chakra.

When this exercise begins to take effect the area of your perineum
will begin to feel hot; at the same time a similar sensation will be
experienced between your eyebrows.

CLEARING THE MIND

1   Sit in a comfortable position with your hands on the floor
     behind you.

2   Spread your fingers so that you are aware of a slight pressure
     within your wrists.

3   Bring your head back and begin rhythmic breathing while
     maintaining awareness of a point between your eyebrows.
     On the inhalation imagine that air in the form of white light
     is coming into the third eye. On the
     exhalation it passes out. This stimulates
     the pituitary gland.

RIGHT THIS MEDITATION EXERCISE HELPS TO CLEAR AND
FOCUS THE MIND BY STIMULATING THE THIRD EYE.

VISUALIZATION:
THE PLACE IN THE CLOUDS

Allow this place to dissolve and find yourself standing within an open, circular balcony. Feel a soft breeze on your face. You are standing on a balcony at the top of a high tower. You do not know how you found yourself here; it does not matter. You look out from your eyrie. Your vantage point is so high that clouds swirl beneath you. Here, you are above the clouds. The sky is bright and clear with an unfamiliar clarity. In the sky hangs a bright sun. You look down upon the clouds that hide what is below from what is above. You turn your full attention to the world far below, obscured by the clouds. Yet though your eyes cannot see, you know that faraway life continues as it always has done.

Now you open the inner senses, tuning yourself to the reality of the world below. In your mind images arise, people going about their everyday lives. Below you seem to hear the cry of a new-born baby and then the last breath as someone dies to the body. Now you hear the sounds of love and now the sounds of hate. You watch in your inner mind as familiar scenes pass before you; children play, adults engage in sports, people sing, girls dance, a family sits down to a meal, a group of people raise their voices in worship.

From your vantage point you can see in every direction, you now have total vision, here in this high tower above the world. You walk to the other side of your balcony and allow the inner mind to open again. Different sounds greet you; different images fill your mind; children cry out in pain, mothers weep, young men exalt in the sounds of war, old men wail the note of desolation.

Yet here all about you, the air is clear and bright. You are surrounded by great beauty and there is a sense of infinite peace. This place is so perfect and complete in itself. The sounds of the suffering far below trouble you. Perhaps if you were able to tell them about this place their sufferings would cease. They cannot find you, so you must find them. You make your decision.

Take one last look at the beauty and splendour of the sunlight upon the clouds. You remember every last detail so that you can tell others what you have seen. Perch upon the edge of the balcony and then, when you are ready, leap into the air.

TIPS FOR WORKING WITH THE BROW CHAKRA

DREAM IMAGES

This level of consiousness transcends the dream state; it is beyond the realm of dreaming.

BACH FLOWER REMEDIES

Beech	3	Tolerance
Cerato	5	Following the inner guide
Chestnut bud	7	Being open to learning from life
Gentian	12	Acceptance
Olive	23	Trusting cosmic harmony
Walnut	33	Being able to listen to the inner voice

MUSIC

Use music to stimulate your natural ability to visualize.
Enter a piece of music and allow scenes and images spontaneously to appear in the mind's eye. Try listening to *Freefall* by Malcolm Harrison, *Cascade* by Terry Oldfield or *Inner Harmony* by Arden Wilkin.

LEFT THE CERATO BACH FLOWER REMEDY CAN HELP TO BRING YOU INTO CONTACT WITH YOUR INNER GUIDE.

Your descent is slow. As you fall keep reminding yourself of the need to remember what you have seen. As you fall so the light fades and dims. The sense of clarity passes. Everything seems to become hazy as you descend. There is only silence now, but you know you will find the children, the young boys, the women and the men. You hope that you have not forgotten what you came to tell them.

THE GATEWAY
OF THE VOID

CHAPTER TEN

We now reach our destination. We have arrived at the final chakra and our journey is complete. We have reached the sahasrara chakra, which is represented as a multi-layered lotus of a thousand white petals. Each layer is inscribed with 50 Sanskrit letters and the petals cling closely to the head to symbolize the cosmic forces which now descend like a shower upon the individual.

FUNCTIONS OF THE CROWN CHAKRA

The sahasrara chakra is unique among the chakras. It has neither a bija mantra nor an elemental attribution. Its functions and attributes are described by its thousand petals and by the symbols contained within the pericarp of the lotus. Here we find mandalas of the sun and moon, surya and chandra respectively. The solar and lunar currents have been present throughout the journey as ida and pingala. These twin forces were absorbed into the sushumna at the brow chakra. Now their final destination is revealed. Within the mandala of the moon is a lightning-like triangle. This is described as being as fine as the hundredth part of a lotus fibre. Within this is the Nirvana-Kala. Within Nirvana-Kala is the para bindu which is both Shiva and Shakti. Within the bindu is the void.

THE CROWN CHAKRA: TABLE OF CORRESPONDENCES

LOCATION: Crown of head

SANSKRIT NAME: Sahasrara, meaning 'thousandfold'

ELEMENT: None applicable

FUNCTION: Union

INNER STATE: Bliss

BODY PARTS: Cerebral cortex, brain, the whole body

GLAND: Pineal

MALFUNCTION: Alienation

COLOUR: Violet

SOUND: None applicable

SENSE: None applicable

ANIMALS: The risen serpent

DEITIES: Shiva

ABOVE THE HINDU GOD SHIVA, THE CORRESPONDENT DEITY OF THE CROWN CHAKRA.

These images are rather like Russian dolls residing one within the other. The difference is that of scale and meaning. We are asked to imagine the infinitesimal manifesting the infinitely great. We are confronted by the microcosmic and the macrocosmic: the void is smaller than the thousandth part of a hair yet it is also 'the chief root of Liberation'.

The images and symbols for this chakra represent that which is beyond rational understanding. Words are only pointers towards the experience of reality which defies description.

Sahasrara means thousandfold. This symbolizes the totality of creation. This centre carries the total sound potential of the whole Sanskrit alphabet; 50 letters are inscribed on each of the 20 layers. The whole image is designed to convey the idea of wholeness, completion and realization.

LOCATION OF THE CROWN CHAKRA

This centre is located four finger-breadths above the crown of the head. If you are sensitive, you can feel the presence of this chakra by holding your hand with a flat palm above the top of the head for a few moments. Even after the hand has been moved away there is a tingling or prickling sensation which emanates from above the head but can also be felt at the top of the head. This is a highly sensitive area in individuals who have opened this chakra even to a small degree. The Christian tradition unconsciously recognizes the same state of spiritual purity through its art and iconography. Saints and great teachers are invariably depicted with a halo of golden light about the head. This convention of religious art is now so deeply embedded that it is rarely seen for what it is: the accurate, if stylized, depiction of the awakened crown chakra itself. A halo of light is not just a piece of artistic fancy.

THE ABODE OF SHIVA

The crown chakra is called The Abode of Shiva. It is the goal of the risen Kundalini, the place where Shiva and Shakti unite. It is the place of union where the marriage is celebrated. Shakti, mother of form, rises to meet Shiva, consciousness. Two opposite yet mutually attractive powers meet and coalesce. The union of the opposites is a recurrent theme in alchemy. The partners are referred to as the king and queen or as sol and luna. These opposing forces are finally united after the completion of separate purification and transformation processes. This state brings final liberation from the wheel of rebirth. Rebirth can serve no purpose when there is no longer any sense of self. Reincarnation is classically viewed as a means whereby consciousness is slowly released from numerous imprisoning illusions. When this task has been accomplished, consciousness is liberated or enlightened.

The level of consciousness represented by the awakened crown chakra is itself the crowning achievement of the human condition. The cycle of rebirth which impels consciousness back into incarnation over and over again is finally transcended. All spiritual systems point towards an ultimate goal or final point. The goal of Yoga is union. In Hinduism, it is called moksha-liberation. In Buddhism it is called Nirvana, cessation of desire. In Sufism it is called baqa, union with God. The awakening of the crown chakra is at the heart of these ultimate experiences.

WORKING WITH THE CROWN CHAKRA

Exercises, techniques and methods for working with the sahasrara chakra are often withheld by teachers who are willing to give practical methods for the other chakras. Some teachers take the view that no techniques can be given because the sahasrara is beyond such a mechanical approach. It also seems likely that instructions are preserved within oral teaching traditions where there is no chance of abuse or misunderstanding. The most important factor in the awakening of the sahasrara chakra is genuine dedication, which sustains the individual through long-term spiritual practice and brings inner guidance when there is no external teacher.

ABOVE THE AWAKENING OF CONSCIOUSNESS LOCATED IN THE CROWN CHAKRA IS THE SAME AS THE BUDDHIST SPIRITUAL GOAL OF ENLIGHTENMENT.

111

The image of the lotus is itself a symbolic representation of the nature of the human being. The lotus roots in the mud but flowers in the air at the surface of the water. The sahasrara chakra is represented by the beautiful bloom with its many petals opening upon the head of the individual. The crown chakra represents the potential for enlightenment that we all possess. The sevenfold pattern represented by the chakra system is the blueprint for spiritual development.

ASANAS

HEADSTAND (SALAMBASIRSASANA)

The headstand is called the king of postures.
Begin by working against a wall for support.

1 Make a pad with a folded blanket.
2 Kneel facing the wall. Interlock your fingers
  and cup your head in the hands.
3 Place your interlocked hands firmly on the
  blanket. Make sure that your wrists and
  forearms are strong. Straighten your legs
  and begin to walk your feet in towards
  the wall until your shoulders make
  contact with the wall. Kick up
  with your feet.

ABOVE THE HEADSTAND ASANA HELPS TO
STIMULATE THE THIRD EYE CHAKRA.

THE COMMUNION OF LIGHT

1 Sit with a straight spine.
2 Raise prana from the muladhara up to the sahasrara in a steady
  stream of light. Do this on a long inbreath.
3 Imagine an aperture opening at the top of your head. Let the
  energy stream out into the universe.
4 Visualize this energy merging with the source of all life in
  whatever way you conceive this.
5 On the exhalation absorb prana through the top of your head.
  Let it descend to the muladhara. Merge this with the pool of

prana at the base of your spine by imagining the two forces coalescing into one.

6   Repeat the pattern of inhalation and exhalation.

THOUSAND-PETALLED LOTUS MEDITATION

1   Sit comfortably with a straight spine, rest your hands on your knees. Connect the tips of your thumbs and index fingers.

2   Imagine a lotus at the top of your head. At first its petals are tightly closed. Watch as the petals begin to unfold until the lotus is as open as possible. As the lotus opens you may hear a sound resonating internally; you may see swirling colours or feel an influx of energy through the top of the head.

3   Imagine that the lotus is bathed in a shaft of light. Inhale and draw energy down through the lotus. On the exhalation fill each of the chakras in descending order. If you do not feel confident enough to visualize the whole sequence, hold the energy in one chakra on the first day. Build up the sequence by adding one chakra a day at a time. It is worth spending time to master this exercise. When completed the whole body feels energized. It is helpful in awakening and cleansing the other chakras.

SEVEN-FOLD BREATH

1   Sit with a straight back.

2   Raise prana from the muladhara into the top of your head and exhale.

3   On next inhalation let it descend to the ajna. Hold it at the ajna by retaining your breath momentarily and exhale.

4   On the next inhalation let it fall to the vishuddi. Hold it at the vishuddi by retaining the breath momentarily and exhale.

5   Repeat with each of the chakras. When you reach the muladhara repeat the sequence and raise prana to the top of the head again. This is an excellent exercise for learning to control the flow of prana. It sharpens the inner sight and develops sensitivity to the

personal flow of energies. It is not appropriate to suggest Bach flower remedies, or music for this chakra. Instead let us end with some words from the *Siva Samhita.*

Thus constantly practising the self-luminous becomes manifest; here end all the teachings of the Guru (they can help the student no further). Henceforth he (she) must help himself (herself), they can no more increase his (her) reason or power; henceforth by the mere force of his (her) own practice he (she) must gain the Gnosis.

THE TEMPLE
OF THE LOTUS

It is important that we have the right attitude to chakra awakening. We should treat our work with reverence and care. Chakra work should not be undertaken lightly nor out of idle curiosity but out of a genuine commitment to the process of self-awareness and self-realization.

115

RITUAL WORK

To underline the significance and value that we place upon the process, we can make chakra awakening the focal point for ritual work. When we ritualize a process we accord it a special place in our lives. The ritual form takes the work away from the context of the mundane. It provides a space where all the senses are totally immersed in a concentrated atmosphere. We may use colour, poetry, sacred text invocation, chanting and meditation to build the Temple of the Lotus.

The preparation and necessary organization which are required for any ritual, whether for a group or a single individual serve to focus all the energies upon the purpose of the work. If we undertake chakra work purely as an intellectual exercise we will certainly fail.

To prepare a ritual based on one of the chakras, first understand as much about the chakra as possible. Use this as the structure for your ritual. A great deal of prior organization is required if a ritual is going to flow smoothly. Begin by deciding which chakra you wish to focus upon.

Prepare the traditional representation of the relevant chakra by painting the symbols in the appropriate colours. If you are not happy with this, select another way of representing the chakra. You might like to represent the deities of the chakra separately with a picture or other symbol. The purpose of this is to focus the whole of your energies upon the work in hand. When you have prepared these you will need to decide upon the form of the ritual and the words that will be used.

Any ritual has a number of stages: the opening, the calling of energies, the assimilation of energies, the sending forth of energies and the closing.

RITUAL FOR THE BASE CHAKRA

The following is a suggested framework for working with the muladhara chakra. It can be expanded or disregarded; it serves only as an example.

Prepare an altar with a red cloth. On the cloth there should be a candle, the prepared image for the muladhara chakra, images or symbols for the god-forms that you have chosen to work with and any other items that will be called upon.

Create a circle according to your chosen tradition. You might walk around the space three times or you might open your circle by addressing each of the quarters in turn. When your circle is

LEFT WHEN YOU PERFORM A CHAKRA RITUAL, CREATE AN ALTAR ADORNED WITH A CANDLE AND APPROPRIATE IMAGES AND SYMBOLS.

created, light the candle on the altar to signify that the work has begun. Accompany this act with a statement which places your work under the auspices of the powers that you choose to work with. If you do not wish to name specific forces, open with a general statement such as, 'Let this place be opened in the name of the forces of Life and Light.'

Now you must set the work in motion by mobilizing the group mind, which represents the unified mind of all those present into a single force. State your intention clearly, 'We meet to celebrate the powers of earth, to find the roots which intertwine, to establish the foundation which holds us firm.' You might like to open with appropriate music such as tribal drumming. If space permits have group dancing, which will liberate personal energies.

Bring the relevant correspondences to bear one at a time. Accompany each with poetry, prose or sacred text. Aim simply to bring out the meaning of each of the qualities of the chakra.

Here is red, river of life,
Attendant at birth, still at death.
Red for our passions, red for our life,
Roused beyond measure in our struggle to survive.

This section can be as simple or as elaborate as you wish. You could have something red on the altar as a focal point; you could light a red candle or arrange to switch the room lighting to red at this point.

Move through each of the qualities of the chakra in turn. Elemental earth can be represented by physical earth, a stone, or a small living plant. Speak about the earth which is home to us all. Draw the group mind to consider the yantra and to Airavata, the elephant of Indra. When you have spoken on the nature of all the appropriate symbols you might like to ask a blessing from the presiding deities. Ask for whatever you feel you need from this chakra. Now the group can move on to the more dynamic aspects of mantra and meditation. Use the bila mantra for a period of group chanting. Then move on to a guided meditation or provide a silent time for individual reflection. Finally let each participant receive an appropriate gift. This could be a seed, a crystal or perhaps a red stone. This not only encapsulates the individual experience but also represents the energies being taken out into the world.

ABOVE A GIFT OF A CRYSTAL TO THE PARTICIPANTS SIGNIFIES THE CHAKRA ENERGIES FLOWING INTO THE WORLD.

Close the session by reversing your opening format. Offer thanks to any supra-mundane forces that you have called into the circle and extinguish the central candle. 'Our work is done. Let us return to the outer world. Let each depart in peace one with another.'

After the ritual provide refreshment. This literally helps to bring people back to earth. It is helpful if all the participants prepare a written report on the work. This feedback enables individuals to explore their own reactions. The group report creates a total picture of all the shared experiences and can be helpful for planning future rituals. If the group meets on a regular basis the participants will naturally be able to share the longer-term effects of the work with each other. There are no hard and fast rules for writing a ritual except that its effectiveness will be directly proportional to the effort invested in it. The preparation period can be fruitful and illuminating. It is as important as the actual experience of the ritual. Ritual can be thought of as symbolism in activity. The circle is a dynamic three-dimensional mandala which brings symbolic values to life. It is truly the alchemical retort in which individuals may be transformed and reborn.

Glossary

Abhayamudra The hand gesture of dispelling fear.

Agni The god of fire, related to the solar plexus chakra.

Airavata The elephant of Indra, which emerged from the churning of the ocean, related to the base chakra.

Ajna chakra The brow chakra.

Akasa Spirit, ether, the fifth element.

Anahata chakra The heart chakra.

Anamaya kosa The food-formed sheath of the gross body.

Anandakanda lotus The subsidiary centre of the heart chakra having eight petals; this is the home of the celestial wishing tree.

Apana One of the five forms of prana.

Applied kinesiology The science of muscle activation.

Asanas The physical postures of Yoga.

Astral body (or field) The astral aspect of the aura.

Atma puri The city of the soul consisting of the physical and etheric levels together.

Aura The energy field emanated by the living form.

Bija mantra The seed sound of each chakra embodied in the mantra.

Binah The third sephirah of the Tree of Life corresponding, jointly with Hokmah, to the ajna chakra.

Binda A point of energy ready for creation.

Bodhissatva 'Wisdom-bearing'; one who is enlightened.

Causal body (or field) The aspect of being that is based in the causal, universal level.

Chakra 'Wheel'; the centres of living energy in the subtle body.

Chesed The fourth sephirah of the Tree of Life reflected along with Geburah and Tiphareth, in the heart chakra.

Citrini The inner-most channel of the sushumna meridian.

Dakini The Sakti or energy of the base chakra.

Esoteric The inner path of spiritual practice.

Etheric A level of subtle energy which interpenetrates all physical matter.

Exoteric The outer path of religious observance.

Gauri 'The eternal'; the great mother; deity of the throat chakra.

Geburah The fifth sephirah of the Tree of Life reflected, along with Tiphareth and Chesed in the heart chakra.

Goraknath A tenth century sage and author of the *Gorakshashatakam*, a treatise on chakra awakening.

Granthi Knot or junction of energy streams on the subtle body found at the base, heart and brow chakras, called the Brahma, Vishnu and Rudra knots respectively.

Hakini The Sakti or energy of the brow chakra.

Hod The eighth sephirah of the Tree of Life corresponding, jointly with Netzach, to the solar plexus chakra.

Hokmah The second sephirah of the Tree of Life corresponding, jointly with Binah, to the ajna chakra.

Ida The lunar current that starts at the left side of the base chakra and terminates at the right nostril; also called Chandra or the Ganges River.

Indra 'Strong and mighty'; the supreme god in the Vedic pantheon

Jalandhara banda The neck lock, used to affect the flow of Kundalini energy in the body.

Kakini The Sakti or energy of the heart chakra.

Karma Action, the law of cause and effect that binds consciousness to the Wheel of Rebirth.

Kether The first sephirah of the Tree of Life, corresponding to the sahasrara chakra.

Kirlian photography A photographic technique that reveals the energy emanated by living forms.

Kundalini The serpent power dormant within the base chakra

Lakini The Sakti or energy of the manipura chakra.

Lalana chakra A secondary chakra in the subtle body, in the region of the brain stem.

Makara A crocodile like creature related to the svadisthana chakra

Malkuth The tenth sephirah of the Tree of Life corresponding to the base chakra .

Manipura chakra The solar plexus chakra.

Meditation The discipline of controlling the mind in order to bring about a state of liberation.

Mental body (or field) The mental aspect of the aura .

Meridian A channel that conducts pranic energies; also called a nadi.

Meru The spine in the microcosm, Mount Meru as centre of the universe in the macrocosm.

Moksha The state of liberation according to the Hindu tradition

Mulabanda The root lock, applied to affect the flow of Kundalini energy in the body.

Muladhara chakra The base chakra.

Nadi (Nadir) A channel that conducts pranic energies; also called a meridian.

Nirvana The state of liberation according to the Buddhist tradition .

Niyama Virtuous conduct consisting of five practices.

Otz Chim The Tree of Life; the central glyph of the Qabalah .

Padma The lotus, a symbolic description of a chakra.

Padmasana The lotus position, the classic pose for meditation.

Pingala The solar current originating at the right side of the base chakra, terminating at the left nostril; also called Surya or the Yamuna River.

Prana The universal life force that permeates all living things.

Pranamaya kosa The vital or etheric sheath.

Pranayama The practice of controlling the flow of breath.

Privithi The elemental symbol of earth, also a goddess.

Qabalah The esoteric aspect of Judaism.

Rakini The Sakti or energy of the sacral chakra.

Sahasrara chakra The crown chakra.

Sakti (Shakti) The feminine aspect of the divine in manifestation.

Samana One of the five forms of prana.

Sat-Cakra-Nirupana The major Sanskrit text on the chakras.

Sephirah (plural Sephiroth) The ten Holy Emanations of the Qabalistic Tree of Life.

Shiva The masculine aspect of the divine in manifestation.

Sushumna The spinal meridian identified with the governor vessel.

Svadisthana chakra The sacral chakra.

Tantra An esoteric path leading to enlightenment.

Tiphareth The sixth sephirah of the Tree of Life corresponding, along with Geburah and Chesed, to the heart chakra.

Udana One of the five forms of prana.

Uddiyana banda The diaphragm lock applied to affect the flow of Kundalini energies in the body.

Upanishad Hindu scriptures.

Uyana One of the five forms of prana.

Vajra The secondmost channel of the sushumna meridian: also the name applied to a ritual sceptre in the form of a thunderbolt.

Vara (Varada) A hand gesture that symbolizes the granting of boons.

Vayu God of the winds.

Vedas Earliest Hindu scriptures.

Vishnu The divine preserver.

Vishuddi chakra The throat chakra.

Yama Abstention from non-virtuous conduct.

Yesod The ninth sephirah of the Tree of Life corresponding to the sacral chakra.

BIBLIOGRAPHY

Achterberg, Jean, *Imagery in Healing*, Shambala, 1985.

Allen, Marcus, *Tantra for the West*, Whatever Publishing
San Raphael, California, 1981.

Avalon, Arthur, *The Serpent Power*, Dover Publications, 1974.

Bailey, Alice, *The Soul, The Quality of Life*, Lucis Publishing
Company, 1974.

Bailey, Alice, *A Treatise on White Magic*, Lucis Publishing
Company, 1974.

Bailey, Alice, *A Compilation on Sex*, Lucis Publishing
Company, 1980.

Bentov, Itzhak, *Stalking the Wild Pendulum*, Fontana, 1979.

Conze, E, *Buddhist Scriptures*, Penguin, 1984.

Dass, Ram, *The Only Dance There Is*, Anchor Books, 1974.

David-Neel, Alexandra, *Initiations and Initiates in Tibet*,
Rider, 1970.

Davis, Mikol & Lane, Earl, *Rainbows of Life*, Harper Colophon
Books, 1978.

Dowman, Keith, *The Divine Madman, The Sublime Life and Songs
of Drukpa Kunley*, Dawn Horse Press, California, 1980.

Durckheim, Karlfried, Graf, *Hara, The Vital Centre of Man*, Unwin
Hyman, 1988.

Evans-Wentz, W Y, *Tibetan Yoga and Secret Doctrines*, Oxford
University Press, 1973.

Fortune, Dion, *The Mystical Qabalah,* Ernest Bean Ltd, 1976.

Gach, Michael & Marco, Carolyn, *Acu-Yoga*, Japan Publications
Inc., 1981.

Guenther, H & Trungpa, C, *The Dawn of Tantra*, Shambala
Dragon, 1975.

Happold. F C, *Mysticism*, Pelican, 1963.

Humphrey, Naomi, *Meditation the Inner Way*, Aquarian, 1987.

Iyengar, B K S, *Light on Yoga*, Schocken Books, 1977.

Iyengar, B K S, *Light on Pranayama*, Unwin, 1981.

Judith, Anodea, *Wheels of Life*, Llewellyn Publications, 1987.

Kenton, Leslie, *Bioenergetic Diet*, Arrow Books, 1986.

Keyes, Laurel Elizabeth, *Toning, the Creative Power of the Voice*, DeVorss & Company, 1978.

Kilner, W, *The Human Aura*, University Books, 1965.

Klimo, Jon, *Channelling*, Aquarian Press, 1988.

Krishna, Gopi, *Kundalini, the Evolutionary Energy in Man*, Shambala Publications Inc., 1970.

Leadbeater, C W, *The Chakras*, Theosophical Publishing House, 1980.

Lethbridge, T C, *E.S.P. Beyond Time and Distance*, Sidgwick and Jackson, 1974.

Lowen, Alexander, *Bioenergetics*, Penguin Books, 1975.

Lu K'uan, Yu, *Taoist Yoga*, Rider and Co., 1970.

Mackenzie, Vicki, *Reincarnation, the Boy Lama*, Bloomsbury, 1989.

Mclean, Adam, *The Hermetic Journal*, No.31.

Mead, C R S, *The Doctrine of the Subtle Body in Western Tradition*, Stuart and Watkins, 1967.

Mookerjee, Ajit, *Kundalini*, Thames and Hudson, 1982.

Mookerjee, Ajit, *The Tantric Way*, New York Graphic Society, 1977.

Moore, Rickie, *A Goddess in my Shoes*, Humanics New Age, 1988.

Moss, Thelma, *The Body Electric*, Granada, 1981.

Motoyama, Hiroshi, *Theories of the Chakras: Bridge to Higher Consciousness*, Theosophical Publishing House, 1988.

Parfitt, Will, *The Living Qabalah,* Element Books, 1988.

Powell, A E, *The Etheric Double*, Theosophical Publishing House, 1979.

Radha Sivananda, Swami, *Kundalini Yoga for the West*, Shambala Publications Inc., 1978.

Radice, Betty, ed., *The Upanishads*, Penguin, 1985.

Rawson, Philip, *Tantra*, Thames and Hudson, 1973.

Rendel, Peter, *Introduction to the Chakras*, 1977.

Robertson, Olivia, *The Call of Isis*, Cesara Publications, 1975.

Ross & Wilson, *Anatomy and Physiology in Health and Illness*, Churchill Livingstone, 1987.

Satprem, *Sri Aurobindo, or the Adventure of Consciousness*, Harper and Row, 1968.

Satyananda, Paramahamsa, *Pranya Vidya*, International Yoga Fellowship, 1976.

Scott, Mary, *Kundalini in the Physical World*, Routledge & Kegan Paul, 1983.

Sherwood, Keith, *Chakra Therapy for Personal Growth and Healing*, Llewellyn Publications, 1988.

Shuttle, P & Redgrove, P, *The Wise Wound*, Paladin, 1978.

Silburn, Lilian, *Kundalini, Energy of the Depths*, State University of New York Press, 1988.

Sri Ramakrishna, *The Great Master Saradananda*, Madras.

Stutley, Margaret & James, eds., *Harper's Dictionary of Hinduism*, Harper and Row, 1977.

Tansley, David, *Radionics, Interface with the Ether-Fields*, Health Science Press, 1979.

Tansley, David, *Radionics and the Subtle Anatomy of Man*, Health Science Press, 1976.

Thie, John F., *Touch for Health*, DeVorss & Co., 1979.

Tolkien, J R R, *The Silmarillion*, Unwin Hyman, 1977

Vollmar, Klausbernd, *Journey Through the Chakras*, Gateway Books, 1987.

Watson, Andrew & Drury, Neville, *Healing Music*, Nature and Health Books, 1987.

Wilhelm, Richard, *The Secret of the Golden Flower*, Arkana, 1974.

Wood, Ernest, *Yoga*, Pelican Books, 1969.

Index